TURNING TURTLES IN TORTUGUERO

Praise For Turning Turtles

This is a remarkable narrative, told with none of the stridency that infects lesser environmental writings. It speaks almost in a whisper and focuses on the close-at-hand – the turtles, a man, a village. Yes, it is about an heroic half-century-plus effort to save turtles, but it is really about saving ourselves, our habitat and the future. It is about the importance of education and sensitization to changing a culture and its habits of consumption – a lesson that can be applied to global warming, energy, and so many other complex environmental issues. The writing is clear and engaging, offering a narrative that is informative without being dogmatic, and that blends cultural anthropology, conservation science, and good old fashioned story-telling. Hats off to Anne Ake!"
Ted Gup
Harvard fellow, award winning author, Pulitzer Prize nominee, investigative reporter, Emerson College journalism department chair.

In *Turning Turtles in Tortuguero*, Anne Ake captures the essence of life in a small village on the Caribbean coast of Costa Rica sixty years ago. Readers feel the salt spray and the mosquito bites, enjoy the camaraderie of village life, and admire the beauty and hardships of that past time. We see through the eyes of Larry Ogren, a biology student who Archie Carr sent to the remote village of Tortuguero to study the nesting biology of green turtles. Despite limited preparation, Larry thrives and becomes an inspiration to those of us who have had the honor of following in his footsteps.
Karen A. Bjorndal
Distinguished Professor, Department of Biology, and
Director, Archie Carr Center for Sea Turtle Research, University of Florida

---

Anne Ake's *Turning Turtles* accurately captures the challenges and adventure surrounding the launch of the world's first sea turtle conservation program. Attracted by some mysterious force to the black sands of Tortuguero, Costa Rica, green turtles return by the thousands each summer to lay their precious eggs on this remote stretch of Caribbean shore. For over five decades, conservationists beginning with Archie Carr and Larry Ogren have been traveling to Tortuguero to study and protect the turtles. Turning Turtles is a fascinating journey through the history of this place and the people who have dedicated their lives to recovering Tortuguero's renowned sea turtles.
David Godfrey
Executive Director, Sea Turtle Conservancy

The book is very interesting. In spite of everything I have going on I simply could not give it up. At first, it has a very strong flavor reminiscent of the *Windward Road* (my favorite sea turtle book). But then, it makes great strides toward becoming its own book, its own story. For a Costa Rican sea turtle biologist who began his career in 1987, the year Dr. Carr passed away, this book summarizes a lifetime of groundbreaking work, one that has lasted and will continue to last for generations.
Roldán Valverde
President International Sea Turtle Society
Associate Professor Southeastern Louisiana University

Turning Turtles
in Tortuguero

Anne Ake

Larry Ogren consultant
Foreword by Dr. Archie Carr III

Edgemark Press

Thank You

I am truly grateful to each of the many people who supported this project. Brenda Griffing, my editor and friend, has held my hand—and slapped it as needed. She does not brook lazy writing. This would be a far lesser book without you, Brenda. Without Mark Hendrick to guide me through the jungles of InDesign, I would likely be confined to a padded room by now. Kim Ogren—cheerleader, publicist, girl Friday, friend, and Larry's daughter. Mary Thieme has followed the book from the beginning with friendship, advice, critiques, and more.

Chuck Carr not only wrote a beautiful foreword and shared his delightful writings about Tortuguero, but he read and critiqued the manuscript at several stages. His brother Tom told great stories and dug out old photos. Emma Harrison was a wealth of information and she knows all the best places for food and drink in San José.

Thanks go to Ted Gup, Karen Bjorndal, David Godfrey, and Roldán Valverde for taking time out of their busy schedules to review my manuscript.

My traveling companions on various trips to Tortuguero included my brother Russ and his wife Deborah, my brother Joe and his friend Becky, my friends Mary Thieme, and Elaine Anderson—they said "Where? You want to go where? NO roads!" But they went, and each trip was special.

To my children Mollie Drew, John and Nichole Drew, and my delightful grandchildren Tyler and Chloe: Thank you for keeping me sane and bringing joy to my life. And thanks to my mom for always thinking I am wonderful even when I am not.

Copyright © 2013 by Anne Ake

All rights reserved. This book or any portion thereof may not be reproduced or used in any manner whatsoever without the written permission of the publisher except for the use of brief quotations in a book review.

Printed in the United States of America
First printing, 2013

ISBN 978-0-9911253-0-2

Anne Ake
Edgemark Press
604 E 6th St
Lynn Haven, Florida 32444

Visit us at WWW.turningturtles.com

Follow us on Facebook

Share your stories.

Send your stories about turtles or field biology to:
TurningTurtlesTort@gmail.com

We will review them and share them on our website.

For

Larry Ogren
whose humor, compassion, and great stories
are the reason for this book.

for
all of the Tortuguero marooners
past, present, and future

and for
the good people of Tortuguero village

Foreword

WHAT FOLLOWS IS not one story but three, artfully braided together by the author into a single narrative. It is the story of a young man, Larry Ogren; the story of a community, the village of Tortuguero in Costa Rica; and the story of an evolving scientific program, marine turtle research and conservation. The story begins in the mid-1950s, and it so happens that it tracks the rise of modern conservation and environmentalism. As you read along, it is useful—impressive, in fact—to remember that the Endangered Species Act was not passed out of the US Congress until 1973. The ESA is considered a major bench mark in the awakening of society to the risk of extinction faced by plants and animals on a planet grown accustomed to abuse by humankind. That makes the story of Larry Ogren the story of a pioneer, not just on a remote turtle beach, but in an emerging rush to address the crisis of environmental degradation.

Also in 1973, the world agreed to

Chuck Carr, an active member of the board of directors of the Sea Turtle Conservancy, enjoys growing vegetables and tending bees on the family farm or exploring Paynes Prairie State Preserve near Micanopy, Florida.

adopt CITES, the Convention in International Trade of Endangered Species. CITES was enormously important to curtailing international marketing of sea turtle products, but it would come into being almost 20 years after Larry began his work at Tortuguero, where killing nesting green turtles for domestic and international trade was believed to predict certain extirpation of the population.

It's very satisfying for me to make this sort of analysis of the history and progress of conservation. I've worked in this field for over 30 years, and witnessed parallel tales of individuals struggling to save giant pandas, mountain gorillas, African elephants, and so many others. All together, it is a grand story, and one we humans deserve to be somewhat proud of: At least some of us tried to help!

But, it is difficult for me to remain dispassionate and analytical in recalling the story of Larry Ogren and the turtles of Tortuguero. Larry was a hero of mine. This story begins when I was about 10 years old. My sister was 2 years older; my 3 brothers were all younger, and my father, Archie Carr, was Larry Ogren's mentor! My father was quite an adventurer in his own right, of course, and into our lives he brings this stocky Nordic student with a huge smile and a flair for telling a good story. In fact, with Archie Carr and Larry Ogren in the same room, the scene became a raconteurs' convention, and the family became enthralled.

Larry could also draw clever cartoons, and he would illustrate some of his tall tales with these drawings, further fueling the hero-worship in the Carr family!

What's more, I have walked the black beach at Tortuguero. I was there with Larry a couple of times, and many more, besides, and I benefitted from his pioneering ways

with the turtles and the people of the village. I have turned the turtles, fished the rivers and hunted in the old rainforest, now a national park. I have seen the village rise from a hard-scrabble community of impoverished lumber jacks, to a bustling town, wholly caught up in "eco-tourism,"
a term never heard of when Larry was a young man.

So, I am intimate with the three plaits of Anne Ake's story, *Turning Turtles*. I have known the man, Larry Ogren; I have watched the growth of the coastal community, Tortuguero; and, of course, I have followed the evolution of the turtle story very closely—and with some awe.

Chuck
Dr. Archie Fairly Carr III

Chuck Carr looks at home guiding a boat down the Tortuguero lagoon in 1972.

Contents

Foreword   6

Introduction   10

1   Tortuguero, Costa Rica 1956   14

2   In the Beginning: There Was Archie Carr   28

3   Pura Vida: Life in Turtle Bogue   46

4   Finding Facts: Frustrating, Fulfilling, and Funny   68

5   Flying Turtles and Other Fraught Follies   86

6   And Life Goes On   102

7   It's Still Pura Vida in Turtle Bogue   120

Photo Credits, Notes, Suggested Reading, Additional Photos, Cartoons,   138

Index   140

Shortly after the Endangered Species Act was passed Larry Ogren drew this cartoon and sent it to colleagues reminding them of the importance of beach encroachment issues to the recovery of sea turtles.

 Introduction

THIS BOOK IS not about turtles. It is about people. It is about the struggles and limitations of life and science in the world's longest running turtle research station. It is about a little village that might have disappeared along with the turtles but instead opened its doors to the world. Thanks to resourceful and determined people both turtles and village have survived.

In the early 1950s University of Florida biologist Dr. Archie Carr traveled the Caribbean in search of a favorable spot to study sea turtles. He popped into dozens of coastal settlements and in fluent Spanish chatted up fishermen, asking questions about turtles: How many? How many different kinds? What do they eat? Where do they come from? His search ended on the Caribbean coast of Costa Rica in the tiny village of Tortuguero where he found the largest remaining green turtle nesting beach—and a village dependent on killing the turtles.

In 1955 Carr accompanied by one of his former professors, Leonard Giovannolli, went to Tortuguero to set up a turtle study and tagging station. The next year he sent University of Florida sophomore Larry Ogren to operate the station. The villagers, turtle harvesters to a man, were more than a little leery of these gringos nosing around asking about their turtles. But they were also kind, decent people living on an isolated shore, who knew that survival depended on helping one another. Gradually they opened their homes and their hearts to the strangers. Their trust was well placed. One of Carr's initial goals was to learn how to manage the remaining turtle population so that it could be a sustainable food resource for Caribbean people.

Soon after establishing the research station Carr took a leave of absence from the University of Florida to teach at the University of Costa Rica. He and his wife, Marjorie, packed up their five children, Mimi, Chuck, Stephen, Tom, and David, and moved to San José. Tortuguero became almost a second home to the family—especially to the three older boys, who in the summers would spend weeks under the loose supervision of Larry Ogren or Harry Hirth and the village adults. They lived a Peter Pan existence of adventure and exploration while developing self-reliance and appreciation of the natural world. All four Carr sons built careers in conservation and returned to Tortuguero from time to time to continue their research as adult biologists.

Almost 60 years have passed. The turtle station now boasts several concrete block buildings, a permanent staff, a revolving flow of research assistants from around the world, and volunteers who pay to come and help with the annual tagging and nesting program. The village too has changed. Gone are the unpainted thatched houses—replaced by concrete walls and tin roofs. Many surfaces are painted with colorful murals of local wildlife. The village has become a popular ecotourism center where the turtle is king—more valuable now alive than dead.

No one has done more to study, protect, and conserve sea turtles than Dr. Archie Carr, who died in 1987. The sea turtle research center of the University of Florida is named for him—its director, Karen Bjorndal, is one of his former students. The Archie Carr National Wildlife Refuge stretches more than 20 miles along Florida's east coast, protecting the most significant area for loggerhead sea turtle nesting in the

Western Hemisphere, which is also the most significant area for green turtle nesting in North America. World Sea Turtle Day is celebrated internationally on June 16, Carr's birthday. Most of the world's outstanding turtle biologists began as Carr's students who stepped up to pass on Carr's methods and philosophy to new generations of biologists. For many, such as Larry Ogren, Tortuguero was a life-changing experience. Carr wrote, "Many of the tagging crew members have gone on to high places in sea turtle research, conservation, and management. Larry Ogren who was the spirit of the place during several of the earliest lonely years, is now Sea Turtle Specialist for the U.S. National Marine Fisheries Service."[1] In 2009 Larry, now retired, was honored with the Archie Carr Lifetime Achievement Award.

Carr was a storyteller, and perhaps his most important contribution was in the telling. He saw life as a series of adventures viewed through a veil of wry humor. His books draw readers in and without preaching or haranguing gently lead them to caring about the world around them. *The Windward Road,* first published in 1956, sparked the formation of The Brotherhood of the Green Turtle which, under the present name of Sea Turtle Conservancy, continues to have a huge impact on turtle conservation. The book has gone through many reprints, the most recent in March 2013, and is as popular today as it was in 1956. It was this book that introduced me to Tortuguero. The name was somehow magical and it lodged in the spot in my brain reserved for little treasures. Some twenty years later I met Larry Ogren. He was the turtle guy, and I was moderately interested in sea turtles and their plight. But when Larry mentioned Tortuguero the ember in my brain swooshed into flame and I knew I had to go there.

On the first trip I just wanted to see. I was researching another book and had no thoughts of writing about life in a biological field research station or about a little village that learned to survive by not eating the turtles. But I couldn't stop. I plied Larry with questions, pushed him to tell more and more stories. I reread *The Windward Road* and *The Sea Turtle: So Excellent a Fishe* and searched for articles and research papers by Archie Carr or Larry Ogren. Through Larry I contacted Chuck and Tom Carr. I gained more good stories about Tortuguero and two new friends.

Now that the turtle station is thriving, turtle populations are slowly increasing, and the village has reinvented itself, it is time to recognize the resourceful and determined people who made it all happen. The list of scientists who put in their time at Tortuguero is a role call of distinguished conservation biologists and ecologists. In addition to Larry Ogren, they include Harry Hirth; Karen Bjorndal; Anne Meylan, Jeanne Mortimer, David Ehrenfeld, Peter Pritchard, James Spotila to name but a few—and of course the Carr children. Carr passed on not only his scientific lore, but his ability to say what is true and important in a simple and entertaining way. Several of Carr's academic progeny have written popular books in an understated readable style for the general public and young audiences and all have passed their knowledge and enthusiasm for conservation on to scores of younger scientists.

In the village Larry's assistant and friend Leo and his sister Sibella Martinez are gone, but their legacy lives on. Sibella's daughter, Miss Junie, owns a hotel and restaurant on property near the research station and the family is still the backbone of Tortuguero village. When preparing for a visit in 2012, I was firmly told that Miss Junie did not do interviews, but when my friend Mary and I arrived bearing greetings from Larry and a collection of his old photos, Miss Junie invited us into her home. It was not an interview. I took no notes nor recordings. It was new friends sharing old stories and concerns about families and aging while savoring delicious cake from Dorling's bakery. A lovely evening, a memory I hold dear.

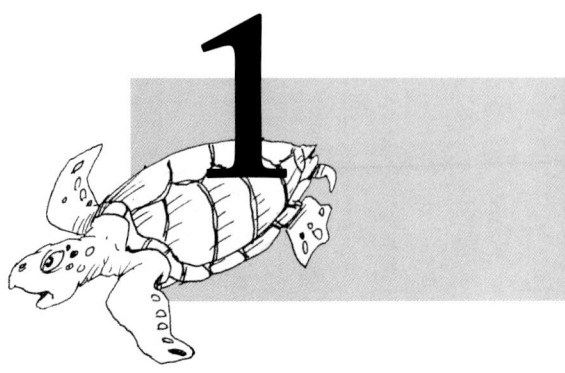

Larry Ogren checks out a green turtle "turned" during the night by a local turtle harvester. The green turtle had provided sustenance to the people of the Caribbean for hundreds of years, and in their efforts to save the turtles Archie Carr and his biologists never became desensitized to the needs of the local culture. Today, as in 1955, the task of balancing immediate human needs with the long-term welfare of people and the environment challenges and inspires professional biologists, volunteers, and local residents alike.

Tortuguero, Costa Rica
1956

THE IDLING RUMBLE of the little tail-dragging Cessna 170 changed to a high-pitched whine. Larry was stacking gear on the beach with his back to the plane. He spun around as it began to taxi. Archie, with his hair blowing in the breeze and his gangly frame hanging half in and half out of the door, was waving cheerfully. His shouted words broke through the engine noise, "Go through the coconut grove, you will find a shack. Bertie Downs lives there. He can tell you what to do. Have a good summer." He called "See ya" and ducked into the plane as it began to lift.

Larry thought, "Well, shit."

So much for orientation, training, and introductions. Larry Ogren was to spend the next few months on this isolated Caribbean shore tagging sea turtles and researching their life history. He had never tagged a sea turtle and didn't speak Spanish. He kicked a toe into the black volcanic sand,

The green turtle was a cultural icon as well as a dietary mainstay of the Caribbean people. In addition, sailing ships from Europe since the time of Columbus had depended on replenishing their galleys with green turtles.

shrugged, slung his duffle onto his back, and marched resolutely toward the coconut grove. When a pack of snarling dogs rushed him from Bertie's camp beneath the palms, Larry, a man not given to vulgar language, uttered another "Shit!"

Larry's contact, Bertie Downs, was a large Nicaraguan with a mysterious past; he lived in a thatched house on the Tortuguero peninsula and farmed coconuts. When passengers were dropped off on the beach landing strip or walked down from Barra del Colorado, he charged a small fee to paddle them the two miles up the river to the village. Travelers who happened to arrive on a Saturday would be sleeping on the beach that night, as Bertie was a Seventh Day Adventist and never worked on his church's Sabbath. Archie, recalling that detail, had made sure that Larry arrived in the middle of the week.

After Bertie had calmed his dogs, he helped Larry load his belongings in a dugout canoe called a cayuca. Larry later wrote to his mother, "My god, was that something, all loaded down in that tippy, hacked-out, dug out with all my bags! Then it started to rain on top of that."

Powerful muscles rippled in strong black arms as Bertie propelled the cayuca toward the village. As rain soaked through his clothes, Larry scanned the water and the surrounding jungle seeking crocodiles and colorful jungle birds. He couldn't believe his luck to be here. Just a few weeks before, he was in Gainesville, Florida, walking a crowded hallway in the biology building of the University of Florida (UF). Dr. Archie Carr approached him. Larry knew who Dr. Carr was—everyone in the biology department did. Carr said, "You Ogren?" Puzzled,

> **BERTIE DOWNS**
>
> In April of 1982 Bertie Downs was murdered. Two strangers, one a Panamanian and one a Costa Rican, came to the village and hung around for a few days taking unfair advantage of village hospitality. Then they began to steal things. They made their way down the peninsula to Bertie's coconut grove and brutally killed him, perhaps for defending his property. Harry Lefever, the author of *Turtle Bogue*, writes that Bertie had a son, Sam Hudson, who lived in Barra del Colorado. Mr. Hudson offered a brief, blunt, yet loving summation of his father's life and death: "He was old. I think he had eighty-seven years. But he was strong yet, you know. Two of them did that, tied him up, like you tie a pig. Sad. He was a nice guy—and strong. He was made of good material, like the old-time Atlas Motors."

Larry nodded that he was. Carr continued, "I hear you like snakes, is that right?" Larry confirmed that he did like snakes. Then Carr casually dropped the question that would shape Larry Ogren's life: "Do you want to go to Tortuguero and tag turtles for me?" Larry said, "When do I leave?" Larry later learned that his name had been suggested by his friend and academic advisor, Walter Aufenburg, when Carr complained that none of his graduate students were available to go to Tortuguero. Thanks to that recommendation, Larry was now gliding through the jungle in a tippy boat at the beginning of a new life.

The Journey

Getting to Tortuguero hadn't been easy. Larry recalls that he and Carr took a train from Gainesville to Miami, where they stayed overnight. Archie introduced him to Latin food at a Miami restaurant, saying, "You will be eating a lot of it—though maybe not as good as this." The next morning they boarded an old twin-engine DC3—the pride of LACSA Airline's fleet. With one stop for refueling, they finally landed in San José, Costa Rica. From San José they took the jungle railroad to Limón. Hanging over the rail of the outdoor viewing platform, the two biologists seemed to fly like exotic birds over cloud-cloaked mountains, white-water rivers, and dense, muggy rainforest. In a letter home Larry wrote, "—what a ride. The railroad twists & squirms it's way around the mountains around 7,000–8,000 feet & then shoots down & follows a ravine cut by a river all the way to the coast through the rain forest & on through the coconut palms to the beach & then to Limón." The biologist's eyes glowed with exhilaration as they breathed in wild tropical Costa Rica. They hardly noticed the billowing smoke whipping backward from the coal-burning engine. When they stepped from the train in Limón, they looked at each other and laughed out loud at their sooty hair, ash-crested ears, and eyes rimmed with black raccoon-like circles.

After checking into lodging owned by the United Fruit Company in Limón, and washing away the soot, they walked to Parque Vargas and sat on a bench. Archie pointed out the sloths hanging from the trees. Archie had always been fascinated by the slow-moving mammals. He said he couldn't imagine how they ever managed to procreate at that speed. He kept hoping to catch them at it, to see how they did it.

Moving On

There were two ways to get from Limón to Tortuguero in 1956. You could take a donkey cart designed for use on the abandoned narrow-gage rail lines belonging to United Fruit Company. The sure-footed donkeys walked the crossties, pulling the cart down the track. If you met an oncoming cart, everyone joined in sizing up the loads. The cart with the lightest load had to be lifted off the track to allow the other cart to pass. Arriving at the river, you could hire a man to take you in a cayuca to Parismina. From Parismina it was only an 18-mile walk to Turtle Bogue, as village was known locally.—18 miles with the sea on one side and jungle on the other. The walking was best done at night, for the heat of the day was blistering. Although jaguars were prowling for their dinner at night, most walkers were willing to accept the risk.

The second option was Aerovias Costarricenses a small regional airline belonging to Francisco Vanoli. Vanoli's only airplane was an ancient Cessna with a set of spraddled-out wheels under the cockpit and a tail dragger, a small third wheel supporting the tail just above ground level. The Cessna made one regular flight to Tortuguero to deliver the weekly supply of guaro, a local rum. A little rum helped keep the sawmill workers content, so they wouldn't head for Parismina on Friday night and never return. If you happened to be there at the right time, there might be room for a passenger. To make an unscheduled trip to Tortuguero, you had to charter the Cessna.

TORTUGUERO 1956

When you wished to return to Limón, you waited for the guaro flight, or you spread a sheet on the beach to attract the attention of the pilot of Vanoli's regular run up the coast to Barra del Colorado, near the Nicaraguan border. If there was room for a passenger, the pilot would swing low over Tortuguero looking for a sheet. If a sheet was out, he would land. If he did not have room, he'd fly high over Tortuguero—leaving a disappointed traveler staring into the sky.

For Larry's first visit to Tortuguero, the Cessna was the better choice. Having made the trip before, Archie knew that Paco, the pilot, would dip low over the waves so the biologists could count turtles. On his own first trip to Tortuguero, Archie had arrived in Limón only to be informed that the

On departing Tortuguero in the early 1960s on a U.S. Navy plane, Archie Carr wrote: "For now, I just want to recollect how, that day, I looked back out of the bubble-port of the plane and saw Tortuguero down there sprinkled among the palms and breadfruit trees, more like one of my dreams than like any real place anywhere..."
Archie Carr, *The Sea Turtle*

Cessna was "discomposed." He spent five days waiting for the "recomposition" of the little plane and watching the sloths. When he was quite sure they were about to begin their lovemaking, a messenger arrived to tell him that the plane was ready and the passenger must hurry to board. With a last reluctant glance at the sloths hanging placidly over his head, Archie grabbed his gear and headed for the airstrip. This was the guaro run, so he packed himself and his gear in around the rum. In his book *The Windward Road*, Carr tells about that first trip in the Cessna:

> The little engine skipped and spat, then caught with a roar. Paco leaned over and slammed the door on my side and twisted the ends of a loop of wire together to hold it shut. . . . He waggled his tail surfaces and revved the engine up to 1500 and let it warm there awhile. He tried one magneto alone, then the other one, and it was all the same sound. He held his brakes and opened her up and she took 2000 without quibbling. He looked at me happily. "Everything is composed," he said. . . . He pushed the throttle forward, the airplane shook itself and moved off, and the fat little wheels left rim-deep furrows in the damp sand. . . . I said. "Let's fly a quarter of a mile offshore, or maybe less. If you see a turtle, circle him. How low can you fly?"
>
> "It is better not to splash salt water on the engine," Paco said.[2]

Now, several years later, Larry and Archie were in luck, the airplane was "composed" and ready when they arrived at the airfield. Staying just high enough to keep the salt spray off the engine, they watched for turtles swimming in the clear blue of the Caribbean. The water muddied where the Tortuguero River emptied into the sea, and soon Archie was pointing out the tiny thatched roofs of the village clinging to a long sliver of land separating the Tortuguero lagoon from the sea. The airplane angled sharply down toward the beach. As a group of scavenging dogs ambled out of the way, the wheels hit the sand with a whump and crunched across branches and beach rubble. Paco always stayed in the plane in Tortuguero. He would sit in the cockpit with the motor idling, his eyes on the sea. The narrow strip of coastal rainforest between the sea and the Cordillera Central range of volcanic mountains was subject to frequent and violent weather shifts. If Paco saw fog or a storm sweeping in from the sea, he'd taxi the Cessna down the beach before blinding clouds could engulf it.

Home Sweet Home

At last, after the meeting at Bertie's dog-guarded shack and the cayuca trip through the rainforest, Larry had arrived in Turtle Bogue. Observing his guide's interactions with the villagers, Larry could see that although Bertie lived in isolation north of the village, the big Nicaraguan was a respected elder in Tortuguero. However, Larry wrote, "His language was colorful, but crude; much to the embarrassment of the village matriarchs." Larry was expecting to occupy the house that Archie and his professor and later assistant, Leonard Giovannoli, had lived in the previous summer. But the manager of the Atlantic Trading Company, which operated the sawmill, said he had a room available at the mill. When Larry asked about staying in the house, Don Yoyo Quiroz simply said, "No. You must stay at the sawmill." It was a ruling Larry soon questioned. At night, when he was on the beach searching for turtles, the sawmill was quiet. At dawn, he would drop exhausted onto his cot just as the sawmill began its day. Soon the walls of his room trembled with the whine of saws and the shouts of workers. After a few hours of fitful sleep wrapped in the incessant noise of the mill, he'd get up and begin his daylight duties. He wrote home,

> . . . . the turtles haven't started coming in yet; only two laid so far & about 4 crawled up & then back without laying. I've marked off the 2 miles of beach into eighths with

> poles & white flags & transplanted both nests of eggs to a place in front of the village. Had to board up the nests to keep the dogs out. I hope they hatch out before I leave. Been raining every day so far.

The rain and general dampness caused unexpected problems. Larry wrote to Dr. Carr in August: "I guess I did forget to mention that my feet are in fine shape now. I had visions at one time of all the skin sloughing off though it only lasted a few days and cleared up fine after I exposed them to some sunshine that trickled through the clouds."[3]

Through the summer Larry would look longingly at the empty house on the beach, but when he arrived for his second summer, the house was no more than a mound of moldering bits of damp wood. In the jungle, heat, humidity, and termites quickly claim any structure left untended. Don Yoyo had known the house was too far gone for human habitation.

Turning and Tagging

The previous summer Archie and Leonard Giovannoli had begun work at what would become the world's longest running sea turtle research field station and turtle-tagging program. At that time, green sea turtles came ashore on Tortuguero beach in great numbers to construct their nests and lay their eggs. Hawksbills in much smaller numbers often laid their eggs along with the greens. Leatherbacks, the biggest of the marine turtles, nested here also in smaller numbers, a little earlier in the year. Female sea turtles come ashore at night to nest. Adult males also journey to the waters off Tortuguero, but their purpose is to mate with the females, a goal they achieve several times in each nesting season. At no point in life, however, do the males return to the beach.

After helping Leonard establish procedures for tagging the turtles, Archie moved on to other projects and left Leonard in charge of the tagging program. Leonard hired Sam Martinez, along with a few other local men, to go out to the

Tortuguero 1956

Vanishing Forest

In the 1950s, when exotic woods were in demand by furniture manufacturers around the globe, Costa Rica's rainforests were being sacrificed to fuel the demand. Outside interests were also taking note of the warm, moist climate, the rich soil, and the cheap land. Banana and mango plantations were replacing native forests, and land was cleared to make room for beef cattle to produce meat that would be shipped out of the country.

Approximately 80 percent of Costa Rica's forest has been cut, but today the country is a leader in initiating conservation efforts. Of the remaining forest, 50 percent is now protected as national forests, parks, and wildlife reserves. However, the privately owned forests are still being felled, and illegal cutting on protected lands continues. Deforestation in Costa Rica has wide-reaching consequences because the carbon dioxide released when forests are cut enhances the greenhouse effect, which in turn plays a role in global climate and in weather patterns.

Tortuguero village is now nestled in a huge national park; its sawmill, a scattering of huge pieces of rusting machinery, is not unattractive. Rusting proceeds in interesting colors and patterns, with lush vines claiming the useless equipment as their own. These pieces have become abstract sculpture, speaking of the past without marring the present.

The sawmill. Larry's room was on the second floor far right. His one window looked out over the lagoon.

beach and immobilize the turtles by turning them over on their back during the night—few turtles can right themselves when their flippers are in the air. When Leonard returned in the morning, the turtles would be waiting. After attaching a tag to a turtle's flipper, Leonard flipped the unwieldy female right side up, to begin her slow crawl back to the water.

Turning turtles was a primary source of income for the local men, who were adept at the work. During the nesting season, when the turtles came ashore by the thousands, each turtle turner, or velador (literally: stayer awake) contracted for a mile of beach south of Tortuguero. The veladors took up their stations and watched the beach for incoming turtles. As the females came ashore, the men waited until they'd progressed beyond the tide line, then turned them on their backs and built a temporary low thatched shelter to protect the captives from the heat of the rising sun.

Trussed green turtles stacked and awaiting shipment. (Circa 1950s)

Periodically, a surplus WWII landing craft, the "Bessie," came along to collect the turtles. The crew of the Bessie tossed lines and buoys into the water just beyond the breakers, and the veladors on the beach collected this gear when it washed ashore. They approached each turtle and tied a buoy or a chunk of driftwood to one of her flippers, then flipped the creature back over and allowed her to make her own way to the sea. The crew aboard the Bessie would watch for the buoys and drag the live turtles aboard. There was no refrigeration, and butchering in the moist Caribbean heat would cause the valuable turtle meat to spoil quickly. But the big reptiles could live a long time on the deck of a boat, with just an occasional dousing with seawater on their way to the soup pots of Key West and New Jersey, or to the canneries in Nicaragua.

Getting Started

On that first day, when Bertie brought him to the sawmill, quite a few men were standing around, doing nothing. Larry asked the supervisor if it was payday. He said, "No. They are waiting for you to hire them." Money was short, and Larry could afford to hire only a couple of men to help, so he decided not to pick one or two randomly from the crowd and disappoint the others. Knowing that Leonard's assistant, Sam Martinez, had injured his back and was not able to do heavy work Larrry decided to work alone for a while until he understood his needs better.

Night after night Larry walked the beach. It was usually hot, raining, or both. His eyes probed the darkness, searching for turtle tracks in the black sand. He knew that the tracks, if they appeared, would resemble those left by a vehicle or by heavy construction equipment. But there were no vehicles on this beach. In fact, there were no roads leading to Tortuguero on the Caribbean coast of Costa Rica.

Larry scanned the sand for tracks, then swept his eyes along the incoming tide—hoping for enough moonlight to glimpse a huge turtle riding the rhythms of the sea onto the beach. When he spotted a turtle that had not completed her nesting, he noted her position and hurried down the beach to turn the next one. The nesting process generally is completed in a couple of hours, so timing the return to any turtles left behind was a judgment call, but Larry would flip as many as he could before the night's nesting ended. He would come back in daylight to tag and measure the turtles he had turned the night before and watch for stragglers still coming ashore.

One day he spotted unusual movement in the waves. He

could make out something large and dark, larger even than a leatherback, the biggest of all sea turtles. Upon approaching, Larry could see the outline of a man struggling to beach a huge log that was the perfect size to make a cayuca. The man fought to bring his prize in, but the sea fought back—reclaiming the floating log again and again. Larry waded in and grabbed one end of the log. Working together, the two were able to drag the prize to the beach, though getting it safely out of reach of the tide took the better part of a day. Larry hired Leo Martinez on the spot to help with the turtle-tagging program. Their friendship and working relationship endured until Leo's death many years later. Leo built a cayuca for Larry from the log they'd salvaged together.

In the year 2000, Edna Gail Dases, a Canadian woman married to a local man, interviewed Leo about his memories of life in Tortuguero. The elder of Turtle Bogue spoke of his friendship with Larry and told Ms. Dases a story of their explorations:

Leo at work on the cayuca he is building for Larry from the log they pulled from the sea. While hacking out the center he gashed his finger with the adze and Larry bandaged it.

Tortuguero 1956

Let me tell you, lady, this Mr. Larry had an interest in everything in the jungle. I would paddle him around in the canals day or night. He wanted to touch and see anything that moved. One night I remember silently paddling down the dark canals, when he signaled me with his hands to get closer to the edge of the jungle. He saw two eyes peering out from a lower branch. Well, Mistress, when I saw the two spots next to these eyes, I quickly backed up the canoe, as Mr. Larry's hand was extended out to grab this thing. Mr. Larry asked why I pulled away. Well, Mr. Larry, that thing was the most deadly snake here in our jungle. It is called the fer-de-lance. One strike from that snake and you're dead. So you see, Mistress, in one way, I saved his life. This is why visitors, no matter how much they have studied outside, they still need help from the residents.[4]

Green turtles can weigh as much as 400 pounds, but Larry learned that he could flip one over alone if he went about it right. On his knees between the front and back flippers, he fended off the sharp claws that arm the heavy flippers, which were making broad swings as the turtle tried to proceed across the beach. Grabbing the edge of the shell, he gave a mighty upward push to flip the turtle onto her back. The technique worked pretty well on the smaller turtles; the larger ones, however, sometimes dragged him around. One morning Leo looked at the tracks on the beach where Larry had struggled to turn a particularly difficult turtle and laughed, "You did a fine dance with that lady—all around the ballroom."

Larry drew this sketch of himself and Leo on the bottom of a letter to his mom.

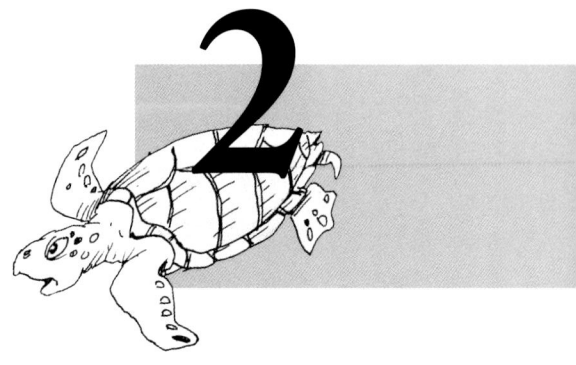

Archie Carr and Shefton Martinez use a wooden caliper to measure the shell of a turtle. The turtle was turned the night before and had been flailing about with its flippers digging a trench around its body. Turning was the traditional way to handle turtles, but as research progressed they found methods less stressful to the turtle to get the data they needed.

In the Beginning There was Archie Carr

ARCHIE CARR DID not go to Tortuguero to save the sea turtles. That would come later. He went because he wanted to know. He wanted to know where baby turtles go, how female turtles find their way to nesting beaches, and how these massive lumbering reptiles make their living. Newly hatched turtles make a beeline for the sea and swim hard—and remain concealed from human eyes and instruments until they are dinner plate size. By then they'd be yearlings, Carr guessed. Where do they go? The question nagged at him. At a diameter of about 10 or 12 inches, which was Carr's idea of "dinner plate size," they occasionally washed up on beaches or got entangled in fishing nets. Where did they spend their saucer-size days, and what was their final destination when

Archie relaxes in a boat belonging to the station. Motors were a welcome addition but were used sparingly as gasoline was always in short supply. Today, motorized boats are commonplace, and gas is shipped in from Limón in 50-gallon drums.

they finally began to show up? Were they world travelers, or did they spend their lives within a few miles of the beach on which they hatched and to which they would return to mate and lay their eggs?

As a zoologist, ecologist, and popular writer, Archie traveled the world studying many animal species. In Africa he wrote of lions, giant pythons, and tiny gnats. But he always came back to turtles. In the early 1940s, he was researching his first technical book, *The Handbook of Turtles*. He wanted to include both the freshwater turtles, which had first piqued his interest, and their giant cousins, the sea turtles. He found that no one knew much about these monsters of the sea. Dr. Carr was a naturalist driven by curiosity. He would have to find out for himself.

He went to Honduras to interview prominent educator Wilson Popenoe about sea turtles. As it turned out, Popenoe knew little about turtles, but Archie fell in love with the people, jungles, and tropical climate of Honduras. In 1945 he took a leave of absence from the University of Florida and accepted a position teaching at the Escuela Agricola Panamericana (Panamerican Agricultural School). The school, recently opened by Popenoe for the United Fruit Company, accepted students from all over Central America. Archie moved his family there and became part of the community. He talked about sea turtles to everyone—students, other teachers, and local residents.

Finding a Home

One exceptional student, known to his friends as Billy, was Don Guillermo Cruz. Billy Cruz shared with Archie his knowledge of sea turtles and his enthusiasm for his home country of Costa Rica. As Central America stretches southward to connect North and South America, the land narrows, drawing the oceans close together. Costa Rica, a wild land of jungles and volcanoes, is part of that narrow band of land. This small country separates two great seas and could provide an opportunity to study the turtles of both the Pacific and the Atlantic/Caribbean.

Costa Rica was known for the huge "arribadas" of olive ridleys, and for smaller numbers of leatherbacks and other turtle species that arrive regularly on the Pacific coast. *Arribada*, the Spanish word for 'arrival,' is used to describe the mass influx of thousands upon thousands of ridley sea turtles, all coming to the same beach to lay their eggs. To the east across the mountains, little was known about the muggy rainforests and isolated beaches of the northern Caribbean coast. But Carr heard tantalizing rumors of great fleets of green turtles and, incredibly, there were hints of a turtle that fit the description of the Kemp's ridley, one of Carr's pet subjects. He had studied the turtle in Florida, but no one knew of even one nesting location for the species. In fact, many turtle fishermen doubted that Kemp's ridley nested at all. They called it the bastard turtle and thought that it, like the mule, was the sexless product of interbreeding between two species. Archie didn't buy the bastard theory and was excited by the idea that the miles of isolated beaches of the Central American coast might be hiding the secret of the Kemp's ridley.

Carr's position as a UF graduate research professor gave him freedom to focus on research rather than classroom teaching. He could travel as needed, as long as funding could

> **BILLY CRUZ**
> "Indispensible" is the word that is most often attached to the name of Guillermo Cruz, an executive with the Republic Tobacco Company. Known as Billy, the businessman lived in San José, where he was always available to extend a helping hand to the turtle project. Larry Ogren says "He did anything we needed, from a ride to or from the airport, to using his political connections to obtain the permissions and permits we needed." As the first vice president of the newly formed CCC, he took the message of sea turtle conservation to the top levels of the Costa Rican government. He used his influence to bring high-ranking officials to the beaches of Tortuguero. In addition to arranging for the visit of Don Pepe Figueres, the president of Costa Rica, Billy introduced Mario Boza and Alvaro Ugalde to Tortuguero and to the plight of the sea turtles. Boza and Ugalde were later responsible for launching the Costa Rican national park system. In 2004 Guillermo Cruz was awarded the Archie Carr Lifetime Achievement Award. He died in June 2013, leaving friends worldwide to cherish memories of his accomplishments and friendship.

be found, and through UF he was awarded a long running National Science Foundation grant. He traveled around the Caribbean searching for the ideal place to base his research and finally followed local turtle lore to the coastal village of Tortuguero, Costa Rica. Turtle Bogue, in the northern part of Limón province, was in a largely unexplored region of Costa Rica's Caribbean coast near the Nicaraguan border. After an exploratory trip along the coast, Carr settled on the tiny village as a base for his turtle studies and a tagging program. He had identified this beach as the only remaining major nesting site for green turtles in the western Caribbean. A smaller number of leatherbacks and hawksbills also nested there.

Calipee drying in the sun. The dried product is light and easy to transport.

From this research camp he hoped to learn not only where the hatchling turtles went, but where the big turtles came from. Surely the incredible number of turtles that showed up here to lay their eggs didn't live and feed right off the coast of Tortuguero. Fishermen of the Bogue were sure that turtles traveled great distances to reach the breeding beach, but there was no scientific evidence to back up this belief. Carr hoped that by putting some kind of identifying mark on the turtles, he could learn not only where they went after nesting but whether they returned to the same beach to nest again. He began his

RIDDLE OF THE RIDLEY

The Kemp's ridley was such a worrisome item for Archie Carr that he titled the first chapter of *The Windward Road* "The Riddle of the Ridley." As the years went by, he gleaned some insight into the life of the smallest of the sea turtles, but no hint about where they went to reproduce. He did learn that they were known for their belligerence when captured: "The ridleys is always mad," one turtle man told him.

In 1957 Carr and his family drove from San José to their home in Gainesville, Florida with a stop-over on the eastern coast of Mexico to investigate rumors about nesting ridleys. They found a man in Veracruz who said that on rare occasions, a single ridley would be seen nesting. There was no reason to doubt the veracity of this claim, but these few sightings could not account for the number of ridleys observed by coastal people and marine biologists. Mass nestings must be happening somewhere, but where? In 1961 that question was answered. Carr tells the story at length in *The Sea Turtle: So Excellent a Fishe*. It seems that the location of a huge ridley nesting beach had been known not long ago, perhaps by many. The proof was in a film made in 1947—and then lost. In 1961 a marine scientist based in Texas, Dr. Henry Hildebrand, came into possession of the footage shot by a Colombian, Andres Herrera. Hildebrand, who was scheduled to present the material at a meeting of the American Society of Ichthyologists and Herpetologists, invited Carr to come to Austin for a preview.

The informal documentary shows an estimated 40,000 Kemp's ridleys on the beach at Rancho Nuevo, Tamaulipas on Mexico's Gulf coast, going about the business of laying their eggs and doing it in broad daylight! No other marine turtle nests during the day. Though Kemp's ridleys sometimes nest singly on Mexican and Texas beaches, validating the information Carr had received in 1957, Rancho Nuevo is the only significant nesting beach for the species.

turtle tagging operation there in 1955—the summer before he brought Larry Ogren to the village to run the program.

Harvest Time

Turtles were a mainstay of Tortuguero's economy. The meat was popular with locals, but most of the turtles were shipped live to restaurants in the United States, or canned in Nicaragua for shipment to England and Germany. Green turtle soup, favored by Winston Churchill, was considered even more of a delicacy than the meat. The calipee, or cartilage from the turtle's bottom shell, formally known as the plastron, produced a thick, gelatinous broth that was the key ingredient of green turtle soup. Turtle shells were also valuable in some markets, especially hawksbill shells. The hawksbill has a beautiful translucent shell that was used to make tortoiseshell jewelry and combs prized by women all over the world. Turtle eggs were also harvested. They were good for eating and baking and were believed to have aphrodisiac properties.

During the green turtle season there was a frenzy of activity. Veladors turned the females and attached the buoys for later pickup by the boats. Both adults and children raced to dig up the eggs before dogs, peccaries, sand crabs, and other predators beat them to the nests; and the boat crews gathered the buoy-marked females. To increase their catch, the boat crews harpooned male turtles—it was their only opportunity to capture adult males, which never return to land after leaving the nest as hatchlings. But, like the females, male green sea turtles are drawn irresistibly to the waters off of Tortuguero, where mating occurs at intervals over several months. For a short time, males, females, and eggs are all together in one place. For thousands of years this gathering provided a rich but sustainable harvest for both humans and wild predators.

Female sea turtles usually nest every second or third year; each individual produces several clutches of approximately 100 eggs in a nesting season. After a couple of months of unattended incubation, the hatchlings make their way out of the sand. Somehow timing their eruption from the nest for after dark, they avoid many of the diurnal predators such as birds and sand crabs. But even at night, predators lurk on the beach, hoping for a feast of baby turtle. The hatchlings that successfully enter the sea find marine predators waiting with open jaws. For millennia, the large number of eggs laid by each female turtle provided food for many other creatures,

while assuring that enough of the newborns survived to maintain the turtle population. There were enough eggs to sustain a stable turtle population and to provide a protein feast for many predators, including humans.

Archie Carr enjoyed a good turtle stew or turtle fin soup as much as the next man. And in the early 1950s, there was still an abundance of turtles. He saw turtle products

Harry Hirth measures a turtle's head as Archie takes notes and Larry looks on. An unidentified man watches in the background as a sustainable resource if they were harvested responsibly. Every year, the turtles arrived right on schedule. After the nesting season, they disappeared. But the next year turtles again appeared by the thousands to nest on the beaches of Tortuguero and other beaches around the world. It had always been so.

These men likely came down from Barra del Colorado or possibly Nicaragua to hunt the hawksbills that hung out on the rocky bottom around Tortuguero. Hawksbills were not eaten, but were taken for their valuable shells.

Changing Viewpoint

Carr's initial goal had been to unravel the secrets of the life of the sea turtle. But, after seeing the slaughter and talking to old-timers about the declining numbers of turtles, his focus changed. He wanted to teach people to harvest responsibly, so that turtles could continue to be a source of food and income for those who lived near nesting beaches. In *The Windward Road* and *The Sea Turtle, So Excellent a Fishe*, Carr talks about the historical importance of turtle meat to sailors and to the development of the Caribbean. Not only are sea turtles a major source of protein, but they play an important role in the culture, religion, and mystical beliefs of Caribbean people. He respected these traditions and wanted to find ways to sustain them.

However, as the population numbers continued to drop, his focus turned to simply saving sea turtles from extinction. These massive reptiles, which had roamed the seas since before the time of the dinosaurs, were rapidly disappearing.

The native people of Tortuguero and other nesting places could not grasp the idea that the turtles could disappear. They had always been there. Villagers such as Sibella Martinez, who cooked for the biologists in the camp, were incredulous when Archie told them that the turtles might not always be there. He wrote in the preface to the 1979 reprint of *The Windward Road*:

> In one important way the wisdom of the Caribbean people seems to go unaccountably awry. That is in the wide spread belief that the green turtle is an inexhaustible resource. My first season at Tortuguero, when I asked Sibella how long the turtles could stand the slaughter then going on at the nesting beach, she said, "Dey never finish Don Archie. The tel-tel never finish. . . . Dey *can't* finish."[5]

Carr knew that the turtles could finish, because human predation had upset the age-old natural balance. When feeding the village people was no longer the only reason for hunting them and the turtles had become a commodity to be traded internationally, their populations began to decline. The same was happening on turtle nesting beaches around the world. Carr witnessed the magnitude of the slaughter and the egg harvesting during one nesting season after another and knew that at these rates, the turtle was doomed. In his research Archie Carr relied on a resource that many scientists disdained—he talked to the local people, especially the old-timers. In fluent Spanish, he prodded them to tell him about their culture, to share their history and their turtle stories. He learned that although the number of turtles nesting on the beach seemed large to him, it was much lower than it had been in the past. Year by year the numbers had dwindled. After establishing the research station, Carr and his students saw the numbers continue to decline. It was clear to them that sea turtles were in serious trouble.

Carr's quest for understanding the sea turtles became a mission to save them, so that future generations could know them. Through his writing, his research, his position as a visiting professor at the University of Costa Rica, and his contacts within Costa Rica's political system, he would strongly influence the country's growing environmental awareness and conservation efforts. By 1970 some wildlife protection laws had been passed, but poachers were ignoring them with impunity.

A slaughtered turtle awash in the waves of Tortuguero Beach. After the turtle harvest became illegal, poachers took only the precious calipee, leaving the rest to spoil.

In 1975, to make a case for preserving the green turtle and protecting the lush Tortuguero jungle, Carr and Billy Cruz invited a small group of people to visit Tortuguero. The group included José (Don Pepe) Figueres Ferrer, president of Costa Rica, and his wife. One of Carr's graduate students, David Ehrenfeld, later wrote about the visit:

> It was Don Pepe's first visit to the legendary Tortuguero—we had been watching a green turtle nest, also a first for him. El Presidente, a short, Napoleonic man with boundless energy, was enjoying himself enormously. Both he and Archie were truly charismatic people, and they liked and respected one another.

As they continued their walk down the beach the two men chatted, and Don Pepe questioned Carr about the status of the green turtle and the importance of protecting the species. Then, near the waterline, they spotted a disturbing sight. A turtle was pulling herself along the beach, trailing something behind her. The group hurried to investigate. They were horrified to see that the struggling turtle was dragging her own intestines and marking her path with a scattering of eggs. Poachers had cut away her plastron to get the precious calipee and flipped her back over to suffer a slow death. Ehrenfeld remembers the moment:

> Dr. Carr, who knew sea turtles better than any human being on earth and who had devoted much of his life to their protection, said nothing. He looked at Don Pepe, and so did I. It was a moment of revelation. Don Pepe was very, very angry, trembling with rage. This was his country, his place. He had risked his life for it fighting in the Cerro de la Muerte. The turtles were part of this place, even part of its name: Tortuguero; . . . She was home, laying her eggs for the last time.[6]

Later the same year, President Figures established Tortuguero National Park. The biologists who were with him on the beach that night believe that the sight of the dying turtle, trailing eggs and intestines, was a turning point in Don Pepe's dedication to preserving the environment and wildlife of his homeland.

Traveling the Windward Road

There is no doubt that Dr. Carr had a profound effect on conservation in Costa Rica and on the preservation of sea turtles globally. In the preface to *The Windward Road*, his humorous and perceptive story of his travels around the Caribbean, he describes how the book came to be written:

> The appeal of marine turtles for me thus had several facets, and I decided to learn everything I could about them. *The Windward Road* was just a compulsive recounting of things I saw and pondered, including the fascinating Caribbean people I consorted with during the first exciting years of that quest after Chelonia [the taxonomic name of the order containing all turtles].[7]

The book began to build a following before it was published. The last chapter, "The Passing of the Fleet", was presented at the annual meeting of the American Society of Ichthyologists and Herpetologists in 1954. Another chapter, "The Black Beach," was published in *Mademoiselle* magazine and won the O. Henry short story award. An even more momentous event would come from the book. Carr tells the story in the preface to the 1979 reissue of the book:

> But before that a portentous thing had happened to *The Windward Road*. Joshua B. Powers, a New York publishers' representative, happened to read it. . . . He sent copies of the book to twenty influential friends who he hoped would share his interest. They did and the Brotherhood of the Green Turtle was promptly formed with the aim of "restoring green turtles to their native waters, and insuring to Winston Churchill his nightly cup of turtle soup.[8]

The original members of the Brotherhood included Tallahassee, Florida, resident John H. Phipps (known to his friends as Ben) and Jim Oliver, then director of the American Museum of Natural History, in New York City. The group was organized in a spirit of good fun, but with a serious purpose. Archie Carr was named Grand Admiral of the Fleet. Ben provided financial stability, and Jim later helped bring in the participation of the U.S. Navy in a major research and conservation effort called Operation Green Turtle. The group also helped secure grants from the American Philosophical Society for staffing the seasonal turtle tagging camp—the John H. Phipps Biological Research Station—at the Tortuguero nesting ground.

The Brotherhood incorporated in 1959 as the Caribbean Conservation Corporation (CCC) with Ben Phipps as its president. On June 16, 2010—Archie Carr's birthday and World Sea Turtle Day, the Caribbean Conservation Corporation changed its name to Sea Turtle Conservancy (STC). Though the organization had been long respected as the CCC, the name gave no hint of its focus on sea turtles. In this age of electronic communication, it is important for an organization to be easily identified by online search engines.

In addition to the research station in Tortuguero, the STC has headquarters in Gainesville, Florida, an office in San José, Costa Rica, and a research base in Panama. The tagging program established in Tortuguero in 1956 is still operating and still presenting us with new knowledge about sea turtles.

Carr, always a naturalist, took biology out of the laboratory and into the fields and streams and onto the beaches. He wanted to know not just how many scutes made up a turtle shell, but how the animal lived, what it ate, how it bred, and how it spent its day. And he wanted to assure its continued existence. He was practicing conservation biology long before it was the vogue, and he was an important influence in Costa Rica's developing conservation policies. Carr and the STC encouraged the establishment of the national park in Tortuguero. In 1975 President Figueres set aside more than 77,000 acres of Tortuguero's wilderness land as a national park. Costa Rica's conservation efforts have set an international example, and today over 27 percent of the country's land has protected status in categories including national park, wildlife refuge, and forest preserve.

Global Recognition

The future of sea turtles began to look a little brighter in 1966 when Peter Scott of the International Union for the Conservation of Nature and Natural Resources (IUCN) invited Dr. Carr to join the organization's Survival Services Commission, now called the Species Survival Commission. Scott asked Carr to establish a group to study marine turtles, to serve as its chair, and to appoint its members. Over the 18 years that Carr chaired the new Marine Turtle Specialist Group, it consisted of 15 to 30 members from around the world, including his friend and associate Larry Ogren. Participation in this group provided a tool for drawing attention to the plight of sea turtles internationally. Over the years the group has expanded to approximately 200 members from more than 50 countries in a dozen geographic regions.

Turning Turtles

As the turtle station grew, it acquired a name, The John H. Phipps Biological Research Station, and gained structures including a large display board to tell visitors about its mission.

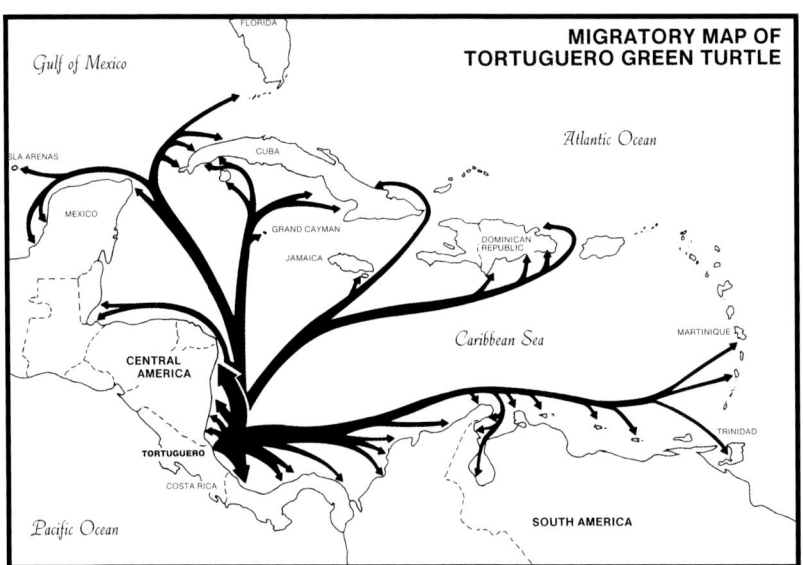

The migration chart shows where Tortuguero turtles have traveled. Initially, turtles could be tracked only by their tags. Today the travels of some turtles can be continously monitored by satelite transmitters.

In 1983 biologists came from around the globe for the first Atlantic Sea Turtle Symposium in Tortuguero. (PIctured roughly L-R) Mario Hurtado, Edward Standora, Colin Limpus, George Balazs, Chuck Carr, Harry Hirth, Njoman Nuitja, Leo Brogersma, Ada Fowler, Merry Camhi, Robert Brundner, Larry Ogren, David Ehrenfeld, Charles Webster, Nicholas Mrosovsky, Jacques Fretey, Willem Roosenberg, Perran Ross, Georges Hughes. Also attending: Archie Carr, Karen Bjorndal, Anne Meylan, Rene Marquez, Peter Pritchard.

A Legacy Left

Dr. Archie Fairly Carr Jr. died in 1987. His curiosity, humor, compassion, and thirst for knowledge touched many lives and lit flames that illuminated the world of conservation biology. His wife, Marjorie Harris Carr, also a biologist, was well known in Florida as an environmental advocate. Carr felt comfortable bringing his children to the village or sending one or more of his sons along with Larry Ogren or Harry Hirth, a graduate student biologist, for extended stays. Tom Carr says he started going to the village when he was seven. Sometimes he came alone and sometimes with one of his brothers. On one of his first visits he stayed with Larry in Leo's house. He remembers Larry as "everyone's favorite" among the biologists.

Carr's sons and many of his students have gone on to build international reputations in sea turtle research and in other fields

Fishing was good in Tortuguero. With the help of an unidentified man, Steve (left) and Tom Carr (center) display a Goliath grouper they just caught.

of biology. James Spotila, a noted turtle biologist and popular author, wrote:

> Archie provided a model for others to follow and a legacy of followers to carry on his work. Most sea turtle biologists trace their roots, either directly or indirectly, to Archie Carr. The older ones were his students or worked with him during their careers. The younger ones studied or worked with Archie's academic offspring. Now the world is filled with Archie's academic grandchildren and great-grandchildren.[9]

The station and the village have changed with passing years, but Larry, Harry, Carr's sons, and others from the first years at Tortuguero still cherish the memories of those early days. Archie Carr's example taught them to be tough and adaptable and to respect not only the natural world but, especially, the wisdom and integrity of the local culture in which they carried out their work. They lived the life of the village and formed friendships and memories they would carry for a lifetime.

Archie and an assistant weigh a green turtle. Methods in Tortuguero were makeshift but they produced a massive amount of data on the life history of sea turtles. More importantly, dissemination of the data awakened global concern for the sea turtles and other declining species. Conservation biology was born here.

With Larry Ogren at the helm, Archie and Marjorie Carr motor down the Tortuguero lagoon.

3

After a successful hunting trip, Albert Taylor, Miss Junie's husband, dresses two peccaries. The wild pigs that roamed the jungles were an important food source for the people of Turtle Bogue—the local name for the village.

Pura Vida
Life in Turtle Bogue

As the Cessna taking Archie back to Limón disappeared from view on that day in 1956, Larry felt a thrill of anticipation. He knew he was the only gringo within miles. He would have to quickly learn the way of the village and live it. There were no restaurants or hotels where he could hang out with other students; in fact, Tortuguero had no electricity, no running water, no sewer system, no telephones; of course there were no radios or TVs. There were no automobiles—or roads to run them on. There was no postal service; but occasionally Paco, Vanoli's pilot, or the captain of the Bessie, would bring a message or letter.

The tropical weather required some attitude adjustment. Most of Costa Rica has two seasons—rainy and dry. Tortuguero, tucked between the mountains and the sea, has but one season—hot and wet. There is some variation in the intensity of the rain, but Tortuguero is never really dry: average annual rainfall is 250 inches. On August 9, 1956, after more than a month in Tortuguero, Larry wrote to his mother.

> Pura Vida translates roughly to "life is good," although it is a contemporary expression it seems appropriate to the ambiance of the village of the 1950's and to Larry's relationship with the people and village.

"Well, the weather is still slightly damp, but it's starting to clear up some now in the afternoon—long enough to dry out some socks and pants and my shoes…"

Larry says you get used to having everything "slightly damp"—it is welcome relief from being soaking wet. Chuck Carr remembers the sour, unpleasant odor and dingy gray look of clothing that had been under continual attack by mildew. He agrees with Larry, though, that heat, rain, rot, mold, rats, and bugs are all part of the adventure. Friendly people, abundant wildlife, "lots of herps" (reptiles and amphibians), lush tropical jungle, a fascinating job, and cooling breezes, make it all worthwhile. Even so, it was hard to get used to the mold creeping over everything. Larry especially hated finding his film ruined and his lenses etched with mold. Not to be beaten, he protected his camera and film with a dehumidifier fashioned from a metal can and a candle. Film was expensive and delicate, and of course, the exposed film had to be stored and protected from the damp until he returned to the States, as there was nowhere to have it processed locally. Thanks to his ingenuity, he was able to build a small collection of village photos.

A Day in the Village

As the sun flushed the sky with rose-colored light, the cocks began to crow and the people of Tortuguero stretched and rose from their floor mats or cots. Most villagers lived in sturdy thatched-roof houses built from odd-sized lengths and bits of leftover lumber from the sawmill. The sparse furnishings were built on site or laboriously hauled in from Limón. The people thatched their roofs with palm fronds. A good thatch roof with a fresh layer added occasionally can last five or six years in the jungle. The thatching provided a snug home for a variety of squatters. Rats, bats, snakes, spiders, scorpions, and a large assortment of insects industriously built nests and tunnels all through the thatch. Their construction projects shortened the life of the roof, and interesting things sometimes plopped out of the ceiling in the night. Larry says, "A lot of poop, but sometimes live critters as well."

For most people, the day starts with a trip to the toilet. In Tortuguero in the 1950s, this meant a short stroll to the beach left bare by the morning's receding tide, where people relieved themselves on the sand. The incoming tide provided the flush and left the beach clean again. The villagers bathed in the river, despite the threat of crocodiles. The sawmill crew preferred to gather on a half-sunken tugboat on the riverside for their morning ritual. Though Larry fit easily into most of the rhythms of the village, he was not really comfortable with the toilet facilities.

Breakfast varied depending on the food that was available. After breakfast, the men who worked for the sawmill went to cut lumber in the forest or feed it through the big saws at the mill. The others gathered their tools and left to fish or tend their plots of cassava, banana, coconut, and plantain. Larry recalls that roasted corn sometimes provided a welcome break from the more traditional fare. The corn was

Shefton Martinez, a brother of Sibella and Leo, arranges strips of turtle meat on a rack and hangs a bag of eggs inside a structure of planks in order for the smoke to preserve them for a few extra days in the moist tropical heat.

> ### Coconuts
>
> Although dangerous when plummeting out of trees, coconuts were a prized crop in Turtle Bogue. Young coconuts, still encased in a thick fibrous shell, contain large amounts of coconut water, a refreshing drink. Coconut milk is a very different substance, produced from more mature coconuts; it was long a mainstay in traditional Caribbean cooking. The meat of the coconut is removed from the shell and finely grated, yielding a rich semi-liquid. Two popular dishes, Tortuguero-style rice and beans and rundown—a stew that could contain either meat or fish and vegetables—were cooked in coconut milk. Pipas, young coconuts filled with coconut water, are still popular in Tortuguero, but the coconut milk dishes are somewhat out of vogue, perhaps because shelling and grating the meat is such a time-consuming chore.
>
> In the early days, coconuts were also valued as a money crop. They could be taken by boat to Limón and sold, or the meat could be dried to produce copra. Coconut oil is extracted from copra, which is lighter and easier to ship than whole coconuts; what is left is sold as feed for livestock. Chuck Carr says he can still smell the sweet-acrid aroma of drying copra that often permeated the village.

supplied by the village carpenter, Chico Montalbán, who also built cayucas and farmed the Bogue's only cornfield. The women cared for the children, prepared food for the evening, and filled a big wooden tub with river water to wash clothes without benefit of soap. They spread the clean clothes on a grassy area to dry in the sun. The children did what children everywhere do—played pretend games, squabbled among themselves, annoyed their mothers, and began to learn the skills they would need as adults.

Dining at Sibella's

Appetite born of long days and hard work made it easy for Larry to adapt to the village diet. Mealtime found him with his feet under Sibella Martinez's table. When Archie Carr first arrived in Tortuguero, he inquired about a place to eat. He was told to go into the village and ask for "the woman who feeds people." He found both Sibella's food and her personality pleasing, and that first meal led to a lasting relationship between the Martinez family and the turtle research station.

Larry took his meals at Sibella's, sometimes alone and sometimes in the company of some of the sawmill workers. As her popularity grew, Sibella added a dining room with four tables and benches to her house, and cooked in an attached kitchen. Since most villagers cooked on a box of dirt that sat on a stand over an open fire, Sibella's cast iron wood-burning stove was the envy of the Bogue. In the beginning, Larry was the only gringo at the table, but as the years passed, Sibella would serve many biologists and visitors to the turtle station. Always dignified and unflappable, she calmly stretched her meal to feed any number of unexpected guests.

Larry remembers meals as being either quite good or very boring. Sibella was an excellent cook, but the quality of the meals depended on the availability of foods. Cultivated vegetables were rare. In a village surrounded by jungle

Sibella Martinez, known for her dignity and strength of character, cooked for the turtle biologists for many years before passing the job on to her daughter, Junie.

and bounded by the sea and a lagoon, there was very little land suitable for growing crops. Cassava, a major source of carbohydrates for many people of the tropics, grew well on small plots in the jungle and sometimes it was the only food available. For Larry though, cassava porridge was high on the list of really boring meals. Breadfruit, the product of a tree that grew in the jungle, was, however, "Wonderful! Boiled, fried, baked—it didn't matter, it was always delicious." Other than that, it was beans and rice, beans and rice: the heartbeat of Costa Rican cuisine. But if the launch wasn't running, even these basics were not always available in Turtle Bogue. Larry started bringing some rice and dried beans for Sibella to cook when he arrived for a new turtle season. "A feast!" he recalls. "But it didn't last long."

In 1957 one of the two launches that occasionally brought supplies to Tortuguero sank in a squall. Larry wrote:

> Now with nothing here in Tortuguero to beckon the remaining launch to come in, it by passes this place like we had the plague. [*Lumber orders were down , so the launch did not have to stop to pick up a load of lumber.*] Consequently, the only way my cook [Sibella] can get any groceries (flour, sugar, coffee) is to walk 30 miles to the south or 17 miles to the north—the two closest settlements. Needless to say I am short of mail, cigarettes, kerosene, etc. But I think I can survive the summer. Outside of the staples, there's some good enough victuals right here—wild pig, wild turkey, fish, bananas, bread-fruit, etc. Oh—turtle steaks natcherly!

Even when the launch was running, if there was meat, it was most likely fish or game or occasionally one of the scrawny chickens that pecked out a living in Sibella's yard. Favorite menu items included peccary, a wild pig, and a large rodent called lowland paca in English; in most of Mexico and Central America it is called tepezcuintle. In August 1956 Larry rendered the unfamiliar name phonetically:

> Leo's still working with me & we have taken a few hunting trips up the river on the side. Got some snakes, crocodiles, [*not for the table, but for research*] and shot some animal they call Tippysquinty. It resembles a rat, only with light stripes fore and aft & a pig's hide. Gets up around 25–30 lbs. Man, it sure eats good as Leo would say. Sibella cooks them

for me — much better than beans, rice, & eggs! They don't butcher meat too often around here, so one has to go out in the bush and shoot game, mostly the white lipped peccary, ...and Tippysquinty."

Sibella's tepezcuintle was one of my favorite meals." Larry remembers, "A thick layer of fat underneath the skin gave the meat an excellent flavor." The tepezcuintles are nocturnal, so Larry wore a headlamp to hunt them at night. The animal's large eyes caught and reflected the light, pinpointing its location. It was dangerous hunting, as jaguars were stalking the same prey.

The best meal at Sibella's was green turtle, the turtle was named for the greenish color of the delicious but sticky belly fat that seasoned the meat and was eaten along with it. The calipee and the fat comprised the most valuable part of the turtle to the outside market. It was used to produce the thick broth that gave green turtle soup its distinctive flavor and texture. Sibella prepared delicious soups and stews from the meat, fat, and broth. Nothing was wasted. When a turtle was killed for food, the villagers gathered around with an assortment of containers to collect some of the bounty. The meat had to be shared, for it would quickly go bad in the humid heat.

There will be meat on the table tonight! Larry shot the tepezcuintle that Leo is holding.

Manatee was also a treat favored by the villagers. Larry sheepishly admits, "I am embarrassed today to tell people I ate turtle and manatee, but at that time they were plentiful and delicious! They were the food of the village and were

TURNING TURTLES

CAYUCA BUILDING

Boats are a necessity in Tortuguero, but with the advent of fiberglass-and aluminum-hulled boats, cayuca building is all but a lost art. Bill Sambola and Albert Taylor were known for their cayuca-building skills. Eighty-five-year-old Bill still spends much of his day in a boat, but he too now uses a manufactured canoe. Not only is building a cayuca a long, difficult process, but the national park frowns on cutting down trees of the rainforest. Cayucas ranged in size from 8 feet to as much as 35 feet. Building a dugout began with the selection and cutting of a tree, with construction getting under way in the forest where the tree was felled. The log was cut to size and the center hacked out with an axe creating enough of an indentation for a man to sit and paddle the emerging cayuca to the village. The only measurement taken established the center line down the length of the log. A cord coated with carbon from an old battery was used to mark the line and the builder was careful to maintain an equal distance on either side of it. An adze, a cutting tool with a curved blade used for shaping wood, was used to finish cutting and smoothing the inside surface. Toward the bow, the sides are gradually curved in to form a pointed prow. Final smoothing was done with a plane. Methods were pretty standard, but whereas some builders liked a rounded bottom, Bill Sambola points out that a flat bottom provides stability.

Chico Montalbán (left) puts the finishing touches on a cayuca (circa 1950s). Alhough some of the work was done with chain saws in later years, hand tools were traditionally used for the cutting and hollowing. To assist in the exhausting work, skilled craftsmen always employed a second, or helper, usually a family member.

considered a necessary part of the diet. And I lived the life of the village—a subsistence culture." After the seriousness of the decline of turtles was recognized, Archie Carr and his student biologists stopped eating them. But when Carr visited the camp, he would occasionally slip down to Sibella's for a guilty taste of his favorite dish—turtle flipper stew.

In the 1950s manatees were not endangered and were an important food source for the people of Tortuguero. The huge mammals are often called "sea cows," because they are large

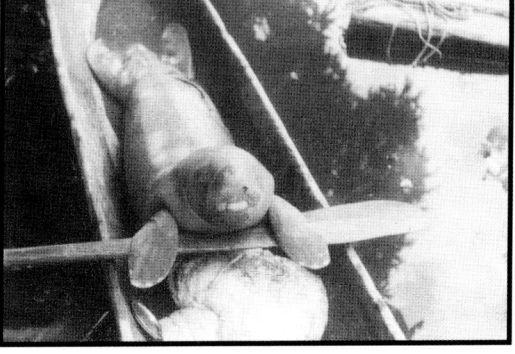

herbivores and because their meat is dark and rich—much like beef in flavor and texture.

Top: Children look on as a turtle's meat and partially developed eggs are divided up.

Bottom: A fetus found in a manatee killed the night before was a boon the villagers would not allow to go to waste. They found a use for everything and shared with one another.

At night the "sea cows" would come into the rivers and sloughs to feed on aquatic grasses growing along the water's edge. Hunters from Tortuguero would go out in a cayuca and listen for the sound of manatees munching water plants. Preparation for the hunt included shaving the blades of the paddles down to smooth sharp edges so they would cut silently through the surface of the water, allowing the men to sneak up on their prey. When they located a manatee they heaved a long harpoon silently and accurately into its flesh. They used the rope attached to the harpoon to pull the manatee near to the boat, where they killed it before attempting to bring it aboard.

Leo poses with his manatee harpoon; the blade is both broader and longer than the type used to harpoon turtles. The wooden spool fitted to the end of the shaft is a float that contains coiled line. The line uncoils when the harpoon is thrown and allows easy retrieval of the implement.

Experience had shown that a living animal the size of a manatee would flop around, possibly injuring the hunters or breaking the sturdy cayuca. Even dead, however, a manatee posed a logistical challenge: how to get 500 pounds or more of dead weight into the vessel.

The hunters' solution was to tip the cayuca to one side, letting it fill with water. When the top edge was almost at water level, they rolled the heavy carcass into the boat and quickly bailed out the excess water. This tricky process required a lot of skill, for if the cayuca were to capsize, the hunters would be plunged into the dark, crocodile-infested waters. Back in the village the manatee was butchered and the villagers lined up with pots and bowls to collect their share.

Moving into luxury

When Larry arrived for his second summer, Leo said, "You will not live at the sawmill. You will live at my ranch." Leo's wife had taken the couple's four children to Limón to go to school, so the arrangement worked well. Larry had Xavier Nuñez, a local carpenter, build a wooden cot frame to support a sheet of canvas he brought with him [Xavier would later build the biologists' first set of calipers for measuring turtle shells.] Larry says, "A canvas cot is the best way to sleep in the tropics. It is sturdy, but allows air circulation, and doesn't get as damp as sheets." He adds, "I had my own room at Leo's and kept it neat and clean—that was not always the case with the rest of the house." A new cot and no more sawmill noise—life was good. On July 29, 1957 Larry wrote to his mother:

> I sure do like Leo's camp, real convenient. Just a few steps and I'm on the beach. No more stumbling through a village with all its barking dogs. The well is just outside the door—nice and clean water—just a few mosquito larvae & bits of leaves—no dead rats! [*On the narrow peninsula, saltwater flowed in and out of the well with the tide. Fresh water is lighter than saltwater and floated on top. The higher the tide, the easier it was to scoop up a bucket of fresh water.*] There is a nice long overhanging eve of thatch—enough for me to hang clothes under it and all. Leo helped me build a privy the second day I was here, so no more hunting around for privacy like last year (which usually ended up somewhere on the beach). Out back is the boat shed with two dugouts . . . a big 18 footer & a small 8 footer. Plenty of ocean breeze, direct through the house. The open beach, well anywhere in the open, is hot as hell, but inside the house is real cool and nice, cooler than Gainesville. . . . Only one trouble & that isn't too bad—<u>rats.</u> They live in the thatch roof and tunnel around & when it rains you don't know where the next leak will be. They also come out at night and nibble at anything you happen to leave out—mostly chow—bananas, etc. But sometimes they'll chew into your gear, clothes etc. I brought a rattrap this time & and have chalked up 5 kills. Also when I sit at the table at night writing, I keep a loaded pistol handy. Then I spot bits [of bananas] around on the rafters. When I hear one come out, I snap on a flashlight & blingo!

When word of Larry's marksmanship with a pistol got out, neighbors began asking him to come shoot the rats that lived in their houses. He used his own ammunition, a precious commodity in the village, further earning popular gratitude. Santiago Conu, however, would come to Larry and ask to borrow a bullet. In the beginning Larry was surprised and would ask, "Just ONE?" The man assured him that was all he needed to hunt wari. And it was. Santiago never failed to come back with meat for the table.

Habla Inglés?

Larry didn't speak Spanish, but most of the villagers spoke a patois English that fell sweetly on the ear, like drops of honey. The villagers were a mix of Miskito Indians, African-Caribbean immigrants from Jamaica and San Andreas, Colombia, and native Costa Ricans known as Ticos. They were mostly bilingual or even trilingual and would slip into Spanish when they didn't want to share their thoughts with Larry.

In his second summer in Tortuguero, a letter written in Spanish came from the Costa Rican government. One of Larry's former roommates, Jim Wing, a language major, told him that it didn't matter how much vocabulary you learned because if you couldn't pronounce words correctly, no one would understand you anyway. So he had taught Larry, not

The hammock on Leo's porch was a great place for Larry to relax after a day's work. There was usually a stalk of bananas hanging nearby for a quick snack.

For Larry, Leo's house was a haven after the open room and noise of the sawmill.

Spanish vocabulary and grammar, but pronunciation. With this preparation, Larry read the letter to Leo in almost flawless Spanish but with no idea what he was saying. Leo couldn't read but, being bilingual, was able to translate. As Larry read, Leo responded with the English equivalent. Leo was sure that because Larry's Spanish sounded so good, his friend had secretly acquired an understanding of the language. Thereafter, Leo was always highly amused when other villagers switched to Spanish with the intent of preventing Larry from knowing what they were saying.

The letter from the government informed the villagers that two miles of beach had been set aside for the research project and that hunting and egg gathering were no longer permitted there. The beach dedicated to the research project would begin at the inlet north of the village and would extend southward past the village. Most of the villagers cooperated, but there was not enough funding available to hire guards to effectively protect the beach from poachers. Some of the poachers were taking turtles and eggs for their own use, not for sale. Meshach Moses, for example, was struggling to feed a large family and turned a turtle every few days during the season. Larry tried to keep Meshach and others like him to the south and off the protected beach, but they didn't always cooperate. In those cases, he says, "I didn't push it."

Leo and some of his children with a clutch of turtle eggs. Eggs provided needed protein, and as a bonus many Caribbean men believed them to be aphrodisiacal.

Pigs and Paths

Wild peccaries were a welcome menu item, but domesticated pigs had higher status as currency among the villagers. Sometimes a single pig would make its way through the entire village as it was traded for a fine fishing net here, a used cayuca there, until someone felt rich enough to butcher the pig and eat it.

Walking through the village with Leo, Larry puzzled over the paths that twisted and snaked their way through the village. He asked Leo, "Why don't the paths run straight? The land is flat with no hills to avoid or waterways to cross." Leo said, "Look around you. What do you see?" Larry said, "Coconut trees." "And where are the coconuts?" Larry's gaze climbed a tree, then dropped back to the ground, and he laughed with understanding. The paths wound their way through the village just far enough from the coconut trees to avoid the trajectory of falling coconuts. Coconuts are filled with liquid, and a thick fibrous outer shell covers the inner shell making the fruit large, heavy, and hard. A falling coconut can kill a person. Suddenly the meandering system of paths made perfect sense.

The Doctor Is In

In the mid-1950s no modern medical care was available in the village. People relied heavily on the herbal medicines prescribed and prepared by a village healer or midwife. The talented Sibella Martinez, in addition to being a fine cook, was well respected in the village as a healer. When Larry and the other biologists were injured, she treated them with "bush medicine." Larry in turn would bring a supply of antibiotics and syringes to the village for Sibella to use on those who needed prescription drugs.

Larry was fortunate enough to stay healthy most of the time, but the possibility of serious injury or infection was always a nagging worry. In September of 1957, he sustained what in other circumstances would have been a minor injury. In the humid rainforest environment, however, the wound site quickly festered into a major problem. Once the emergency had passed, Larry wrote to his mother about it in an understated tone:

> Well Mom, as soon as my hand got better I went right back to Tortuguero to continue tagging. The finger is stiff, but possibly with some therapy—exercise—I can get it loosened up eventually. Oh I had a cut on my finger (little, left) from a turtle's flipper (the back edge is horny & somewhat sharp) and possibly I got it infected when I cleaned a partially decomposed crested guan (a tropical turkey-like bird) that I had shot earlier in the day. It got quite painful & started to spread into my hand & by the time I finally managed to flag down a plane three or four days later it had gotten pretty bad. The Carrs were very nice—they boarded me, footed the hospital bills & everything! They're certainly a swell bunch—I'd like you to meet them next year when they come back from Costa Rica!" [This was during the time that Carr was teaching in Costa Rica.]

Attack on Two Fronts

While in San José for treatment of his infected hand, Larry picked up a newspaper with a headline proclaiming that Tortuguero had been attacked! Even 50 years later he seems disappointed that he missed the excitement. He wrote his mother about the incident.

> While I was gone, that is up in San José, Tortuguero was raided by some Nicaraguan rebels after guns & ammunition. No one was hurt though & the fellas were captured back in the woods behind the landing field the day before I came back. You know that small commissary where I stayed last year, well there was a cache of machine guns, rifles, & thousands of rounds of ammo right below my room! These rebels got wind of it & wanted that stuff to carry out a raid on their president, Samosa [Somoza]. What all that armament was doing in Tortuguero is a mystery! There was only one soldier stationed there to watch about 25 miles of beach!

The invasion of armed militiamen caused excitement that was talked about for years. But there were other smaller, more dangerous enemies. Mosquitoes are a fact of life in the jungle. Sometimes they carry malaria, yellow fever, dengue fever—diseases that can wipe out whole villages. And then there was DDT. The Costa Rican government sent antimosquito teams armed with huge amounts of the pesticide into the villages. As happened elsewhere in the developing world, the teams sprayed the air, they sprayed bushes, they sprayed the houses—inside and out. Mosquitoes died by the thousands. Roaches, ants, scorpions, spiders, rats, and snakes died along with them. Sibella's chickens feasted on the glut of dead vermin and also died. Furious, and determined not to let good meat go to waste, she gathered the dead birds, plucked them, and prepared a chicken feast for her diners.

After the biologists moved into their own house Harry Hirth wrote in a letter to Dr. Carr, "Some malarial crew came and sprayed all the houses with DDT. We now are an official member of the village with our yellow sticker on the door."⁶ It was only a few years later that research about the danger DDT poses to humans and other animals became widely known.¹⁰

Lost in the Jungle

When Archie Carr first showed up in Tortuguero, gringos were a rare sight and not a particularly welcome one. Turtles were essential to village life, and interest in them by outsiders was worrisome. But Carr's easy acceptance of the village way of life and his enthusiasm for the old-timers' stories and the village food—including turtle—soothed their uneasiness. When Larry Ogren arrived in the second year of the tagging program, his good-natured kindness and wry sense of humor served to further acceptance and pleasant working relationships among the biologists and the local people.

Carr's sons were frequent visitors to Tortuguero and blended easily into the life of the village. From early childhood Tom was an avid fisherman and hunter; in his teens he helped provide meat for the village. In Tortuguero, he kept a .38 derringer for shooting rats. He recalls taking the little revolver along on a hunting trip with a rather unsavory

After several seasons, Carr began sending other students to participate in the program. The first to come was Harry Hirth. He moved in with Larry and Leo and settled into the routine.

character that he remembers only as "Boom Boom." Peccaries were the designated prey that day. The cunning pigs can be mean and dangerous, and they will work together to separate two hunters. This happened on the trip with Boom Boom, who made matters worse by shooting and wounding a big boar. The injured wild boar spotted Tom and charged. As the angry pig approached, Archie's son drew the derringer and fired—killing the boar with a direct hit between the eyes. To this day, Tom says, he can't believe that he not only hit but killed the boar with a derringer. Boom Boom gutted and butchered the pig and secured it to Tom's back. It was a heavy load to carry back to the cayuca, but the pride of accomplishment lightened the task.

Leo Martinez, silhouetted against sky and lagoon, uses a machete to hack away the outer shell of a coconut. A skill practiced in Tortuguero today.

Tom's brother Chuck went along on his dad's second visit to Tortuguero, before the tagging program was begun. Chuck liked the village people and the jungles and visited as often as possible. At 14 he spent some time at the research station under the supervision of Harry Hirth, the biologist on duty at the time. Chuck, who stayed with Harry in a thatched shack on stilts, remembers him as a gentle man who walked around the camp singing hymns on Sundays. Every night, the pair patrolled the beach, looking for sea turtles. Chuck later wrote,

> Sibella Martinez, at whose house we ate three meals a day, was a master of preserving food by heat and smoke. This led to more and more potent flavors as the jack fish or turtle roast was reheated two or three days in a row."

Eventually there would be no meat but canned Vienna sausage: "nasty things ... like eating human thumbs, ... tasted terrible."

Vienna sausage on the menu always sparked plans for a hunting trip. Sunday, the only day the turtle team didn't walk the beach, was hunting day. As this particular Sunday approached, Chuck worried that something would go wrong: it might storm, the outboard might not be working, or there wouldn't be enough gasoline. It did rain, but nevertheless, Harry, Chuck, and Leo set out before sunrise in search of peccaries.

> We stashed the guns—cheap but accurate .22-caliber, single-shot, bolt-action rifles—and machetes in the dugout with a basket of food wrapped in oilcloth that Sibella had sent along. Leo took the bow, Harry the motor. I sat amidships and scrunched down in my poncho, trying to be small and dry. The motor buzzed, and with Leo to watch for drifting tree trunks, we slid through the rainy darkness, up stream, toward the Agua Fria, the creek that would take us to the hunting trails. We cruised for an hour. The dawn light came just in time, because the creek became narrow and curvy. With the currents boosted by the rainfall, getting anywhere, even with the engine, meant everybody thrashing around with paddles, fending off snags, pushing away from the bank, fighting a mean little eddy in a hairpin turn. Exciting stuff, and strenuous. Leo waved us over to a place on the bank where a hint of a trail could be seen, an old machete cut, some scuffing on the mud, and we stopped.

The hunters ate the boiled eggs and bread that Sibella had provided. Then, leaving the ponchos in the dugout, they set out with Leo in the lead, moving fast, and chopping limbs to clear a path. After about two hours they gave it up, returned to the dugout, and maneuvered farther up the Agua Fria. They saw large tapir and jaguar prints, but no game. By their third stop it was time to start the long paddle home, but Leo proposed one final attempt to bag some game. They spread out about 25 yards apart and pushed on through the jungle in hopes of flushing something edible.

> I was pretty excited with this deployment and held my gun at the ready with two hands, using the gunstock, instead of the machete, to force my way through any restraining palm fronds or lianas. I was tensely alert, certain that any moment a big game bird would explode from concealment ahead. Through the buttressed tree trunks and understory brush, I could glimpse Harry from time to time, also moving ahead in a stealthy way.

Eventually Chuck and Harry moved closer together and realized they had lost track of Leo. "*Harry Hirth and I were lost in the jungle.*" They shouted and fired their guns, but the dense jungle absorbed the sound. As dark fell, Harry said they should prepare for the night.

> I looked around, trying to define "prepare." There were gleaming wet tree trunks; reddish mud where the leaf litter had been carried off; puddles of water, rivulets of water, and shiny dark-green palm leaves. Far off, a tree branch fell noisily and heavily from some great height, crushing things as it came down. "Cut some palm frond," Harry instructed. "Make a bed. Make a lean-to." That would be the extent of our preparations. I cut big palm leaves and laid them down on a piece of ground that looked slightly elevated. I lay back to test it, and could feel each central beam of each big leaf along my back. . . . The rain let down steadily and copiously. I sat on my harsh-ribbed bed, and inventoried my misery. I was exhausted, . . . a burning of bodily stores not replenished by food since the last hardboiled egg at dawn. I was getting cold too. . . . As I lay there, using my hat to keep rain out of my eyes and nose, my body compressed the palm fronds. They sank into the mud. The water rose up to my buttocks and shoulder blades and rib cage[11]

Chuck spent the rest of the night on his feet with his chin and arms wedged into the branches and notches of a small tree. When morning finally came, the pair renewed their search for a way out and soon found Leo's trail. Leo had cut a broad path lined with gleaming, freshly cut foliage. The path led back to the Agua Fria. After cutting the path, Leo had made his way in pitch dark down the winding log-filled river all the way to the village. The two weary campers knew that Leo would be back and sat down to wait. Shortly Leo's cayuca appeared, followed by five cayucas filled with village men. Chuck remembers seeing Bill Sambola in the lead cayuca. They had left the village before sun up to come to the rescue of two of their own—Mistah Harry and Mistah Archie's boy.

Life in Tortuguero was Pura Vida, both for the gringo biologists, accustomed to a very different way of life, and for the villagers, who had never lived another way. But Tortuguero was destined to change. It would be change wrought not by the gringos who had shared their life but by changing times, the closing of the sawmill, and the decline of the turtles. Yet the village would adapt and survive. Because it was always Pura Vida in Tortuguero.

Turning Turtles

While working at Tortuguero, David Ehrenfeld designed goggles to gain insight into the vision of sea turtles. Dr. Ehrenfeld, currently a professor at Rutgers University was the founding editor of the periodical *Conservation Biology*. The photo was taken by Dr. Robert Schroeder, a turtle and coral reef biologist.

Finding Facts:
Frustrating, Fulfilling, and Funny

Archie Carr loved a puzzle and would worry it around in his mind until he found an answer; but finding answers about sea turtles was a daunting problem. As tiny hatchlings they bubble up out of the sand and disappear into the sea, not to be seen until they are dinner plate size and begin showing up in fishing nets, or foraging for food in the grass flats. Male sea turtles never set flipper on dry land again. Mature females by the thousand, however, appear on certain beaches, where they dig holes in the sand, drop their eggs, and start the life process over again. After laying, and roughly two months before the eggs have hatched, the females, too, disappear into the world's seas.

Eager to find answers about an animal that starts its life buried in the sand, and then vanishes into the seas that cover almost three fourths of the earth, Carr pondered the problem. He had a special interest in greens because of their importance as a food source to the subsistence cultures of the Caribbean. He chose Tortuguero for his green turtle research station because it had the largest green turtle nesting population remaining in the Caribbean.

Carr had learned that some turtles nest singly scattered across many miles of beach, but others nest by the thousands on certain beaches. He saw this mass nesting as the only window of opportunity for marine biologists to have personal contact with mature turtles and, approximately two months later, with their hatchlings. The huge Olive ridley arribadas of the Pacific were hectic frenzied events that were quickly over, whereas on Caribbean nesting beaches, green sea turtles nest in great numbers, spreading their nesting activity over several months. The longer nesting season allows a single biologist or a small team time to accomplish more. The overlap of nesting and hatching makes it possible to carry on adult tagging and data collection while observing nests and, finally, hatchlings.

Biologists had their work cut out for them when it came to accessing all those nesting turtles. Tortuguero is hot and muggy year round. It rains—a lot—year round, and the rains that fall in turtle nesting season are torrential. Moreover, turtles nest at night, and the light of a single match can send a big hen lumbering back into the sea, still carrying her eggs. This means that biologists must walk the beach in the dark, guided only by the sounds of the sea. The gray volcanic sand hides logs, glass, and other beach debris that can rip painfully into a toe. Closed-toed shoes provide some protection, but walking for miles in the yielding sand becomes even more difficult. Sometimes washouts leave behind treacherous slopes or sudden drop-offs into the water.

Two children watch as Larry and Leo tag and measure a turtle turned the night before.

Larry wrote his mother:

> Really get the walking in around here, Mom. At night patrolling the beach I get in around 8 miles or more, and during the day when I tag them I hike 6 or more miles. And when we go out in the canoe, "cayuca," it's strictly arm work—no mechanized vehicles around here! What an appetite I've got now—I hope it will

> disappear when I get back. . . . lots of things to nibble on between meals over on the beach too—coco plums (sweet fruits size of crab apples) sea grapes, coconuts, water coconuts with lime juice [water coconuts are young coconuts that contain a large amount of liquid that will later mature into coconut meat], pears (we call them avocados), a stick of sugar cane to suck on—but not all of them are wild. The limes, sugar cane, & pears Obid (Leo's brother) gives me. And Xavier Nuñas & Leo keep me supplied with bananas.

On another occasion he wrote again about his ravenous appetite and the hard work of turning turtles:

> Golly what an appetite—walking that beach wrestling turtles sure makes me hungry. Sometimes the "old hens" put up quite a struggle—guess they don't like to be rolled over, . . . When they get frantic, they flap those flippers violently & woe to anyone who gets into their range. I haven't been hit hard yet, but I've gotten some "terrific" sand baths. One night I caught sight of a big one as it was retreating back to the sea. I ran out in the surf after her & tried to haul her back. We fought back & forth for a while but finally she caught me with her flipper. Away went my flashlight & just then a wave broke over me, & she took off. They're not all this stubborn, but these are the old girls you remember!

Off the beach, the biologists faced other challenges. In the beginning they had no electricity, no running water, no toilet facilities, and limited communication with the outside world. After several years, they had a thatched roof cabin on stilts built on Leo Martinez's property. They also began to acquire mechanical equipment designed to make life easier, but often it just added new headaches. Over the years, as the turtle team accumulated equipment, letters to Dr. Carr would often begin with an assessment of which items—outboard motor, generator, and electric water pump—were actually working at the moment. The unreliable electric water pumps operated only during the few evening hours that the generator was running. Chuck Carr remembers a big green single-piston, British-made Lister generator that powered a pump that pulled water

Larry's spare time could always be filled with working on the pump, the generator, or the boat motor.

from a well into barrels, which were connected by pipes to the washbasin and shower. Larry says, "The showers were after my time. We didn't have anything nearly that fancy. We thought having a little pump to pull salt water into our turtle tanks was real luxury." Chuck recalls another problematic power source, as well.

> One other little item of interest was flashlight batteries. Jesus. Back in those days, before alkaline, we used carbon-core batteries, and they didn't last long. We'd bring in a big box of them. They weren't cheap. Our lives on the beach depended on the flashlights. . . . Larry taught us that you could pass a dying D-cell battery over a candle flame and restore its power for a little bit."[12]

Flashlights were used to get around the camp and village in the dark. Before the researchers fully understood the effect of light on the turtles, they sometimes used flashlights on the beach.

The scarcity of gasoline was, of course, another big problem. Larry's excitement over getting a 3-horsepower outboard motor was soon tempered by the realization that the engine wouldn't get much use because gasoline was always in short supply. Soon after acquiring the motor, however, he and Harry spotted a big metal drum floating in the surf. They decided it might come in handy and struggled to get it ashore. Like a gift from the gods, it contained 50 gallons of gasoline!

Despite the hardships, many of the world's leading turtle biologists have spent time in Tortuguero—and those who have not, have benefited from the knowledge painstakingly gathered there.

Turning and Tagging

Local fishermen believed that the green turtles nesting on Tortuguero beach came from far away. This belief was supported by two facts: green turtles eat sea grass, and there were no grass beds near Tortuguero. But where had the turtles come from, and how had they known where to go? Archie's plan to put an identifying mark on the turtles in order to track their movements presented its own problems. How do you mark a turtle? You can't just slap a mailing label on its back. The researchers knew that any marking they might apply to a turtle shell would wear off or corrode after years in saltwater. The markers would have to show identifying numbers and a return address, and, of course, they could not harm the turtle or interfere with its movements.

In the first year, 1955, Archie and Leonard Giovannoli used oval tags made of a salt-tolerant metal alloy. They'd flip a turtle over, drill holes in the rear scutes of its shell, thread stainless steel wire through the holes, and attach the tags firmly to the shell. Chuck Carr tells about Leonard Giovannoli's heroic contribution to the turtle tagging:

> But, with all the steps involved in the original technique used by Leonard Giovanolli, the manipulating of the turtle in the dark,

> often hampered by rain; the drilling of the shell; the threading of springy wire through sand-clogged holes; the measuring of the carapace in the light of a dim flashlight; and of course the careful taking of notes— all of that is made almost improbable when you realize that Giovanolli had only one leg! Yes, it's true. He walked for miles with crutches that plunged into the soft, yielding volcanic sand of Tortuguero. And then he confronted the big green turtles and flipped them over. And then he proceeded to drill the shell and secure the metal oval tags.[13]

That first year, there was money available to hire veladors who helped turn the turtles in the dark; then Giovannoli tagged, measured, and flipped them back over so they could return to the water. The number of turtles Giovanolli tagged in a day in 1955 set a record and became the standard for all Tortuguero biologists. If Giovannoli could do so much, there was no excuse for a two-legged researcher to fail to do as well.

By the second year, when Larry Ogren came to tag the turtles, Archie had learned that Dr. Tom Harrison in Sarawak, Borneo was using Monel metal tags. Ranchers identified their cattle with tags made of this proprietary alloy of nickel and copper, which is very resistant to corrosion and acids. Since a cow's ear and a turtle's flipper are both flat and contain few nerves, Harrison had decided the same method could work for turtles. Archie ordered similar tags made of the durable Monel metal, and an implement designed for attaching the tags to a cow ear, which turned out to work on turtle flippers, too. Though much more sophisticated means of tagging and tracking turtles have come with advances in technology, Monel tags for turtles are still in use today.

Birth on the Beach

Although scientists and local observers had long known that when sea turtles finish laying, they abandon their eggs buried in the sand, but what happened between the initial nesting and the departure from the site was a mystery. Gradually,

Finding Facts

Today a turtle's route can be precisely, but expensively, tracked by satellite. Nevertheless, metal tags remain the primary tool for learning about the travels of sea turtles.

through observation and experimentation, the researchers learned that when female turtles reach sexual maturity at between 15 and 35 years of age, they are drawn irresistibly over hundreds or even thousands of miles back to the beach where they were hatched. They don't travel together in great fleets or schools, but over several weeks thousands arrive, alone or in small groups.

The females will mate several times, with different males, and they will produce several clutches (about a hundred eggs) about two weeks apart. This obstetrical schedule succeeds because the female turtle can store sperm in her body for later use. She can also secrete a gooey substance in her reproductive tract that cuts off oxygen flow to the eggs. By "pausing" both the fertilization of the first sperm deposits and the development of fertilized eggs, one female is able to produce several clutches in one nesting season. When the first clutch is ready to be laid, she goes ashore and selects a spot in the sand beyond the high tide line. It is a laborious trek through soft sand for an animal weighing hundreds of pounds and having only flippers for propulsion. She is very skittish during this journey across the beach—light or movement can cause her to make a U-turn back to the sea. When she has selected a place, she uses her front flippers to clear away sticks and other beach wrack. After tidying the area, she digs a shallow body cavity with her front flippers and settles into it.

Oblivious to the presence of bystanders, a green turtle deposits her eggs in the sand.

Now the real work begins. Using only her rear flippers, the turtle begins digging the nest cavity, which extends deeper into the sand beneath the rear part of her body. At this point she is no longer disturbed by activity around her, and researchers can use small red-filtered lights as they measure, tag, and take notes. The turtle, now in a trancelike state goes on with the job at hand, unable to see what she is doing as she neatly removes flipper-full after flipper-full of sand, alternating rear flippers with each scoop. As she digs, shedding copious amounts of salty tears, she carefully shapes and molds the cavity into a bulb shape with the big end on the bottom. Scientists believe that the tears remove excess salt and also help keep the sand out of the turtle's eyes.

The soft, leathery eggs look like ping-pong balls but are intricately complex. The inside is composed of several substances, including the developing embryo and yolk sac. The various fluids and membranes inside the egg allow the performance of such essential functions as providing food,

Why 100?

Most sea turtles lay approximately 100 eggs in a clutch, hawksbills sometimes more and flatbacks less. The females nest every two or three years and lay as many as five clutches a season. That's a lot of eggs. How can an animal that reproduces at this rate be endangered? The Sea Turtle Conservancy estimates that each egg has less than one chance in 1000 maybe even as little as one in 10,000 to survive to full adulthood.

Predators of sea turtle eggs and hatchlings include insects, crabs, raccoons, boars, birds, coyotes, jaguars, coatis, wild dogs, domesticated dogs—and, of course, humans. And these are creatures that prey on eggs and hatchlings while they are still on the beach. When hatchlings hit the water, there are sharks, fish, frigate birds, and other sea birds waiting. On crowded beaches nests are often inadvertently destroyed by other turtles seeking a nesting spot—this is most common with the ridleys, which nest in huge arribadas with many thousands of turtles on the beach simultaneously.

Thus some of the hundred eggs in any given clutch fail to hatch, and many do not survive the juvenile stage. The excess of eggs provides a glut of high-protein food to coastal dwellers, both human and animals. Even the shells and eggs that are dug up and left rotting on the beach are not wasted—in the low-nutrient sand they nourish dune vegetation and tiny sand-dwelling creatures. For millennia the balance had held. One hundred per clutch was the right number to maintain the turtle population and contribute to the food web. But when humans made the harvesting of egg and turtle meat a commercial enterprise, and began gobbling up sea turtle habitat for construction, they threw the system out of kilter. One hundred was no longer enough, and sea turtle numbers began rapidly dropping.

Turning Turtles

oxygen, water, shock absorbency, and the sequestering of waste. Once the eggs have been deposited, the turtle refills the hole with her back flippers and tamps it down with her body. Then, instinctively, she conceals the nest by tossing sand around the surrounding area. When all is done, she returns to the sea to rest. In about two weeks she will make another nesting trip to the beach. She may nest from two to five times, occasionally more, in one season. In about two months, the time varies according to the temperature in the nest, little turtles come boiling out of the sand and head for the sea.

Larry had pieced together information about the structure of turtle nests in the course of moving certain nests to protect them from rising water or predators or to enable him and Harry Hirth to monitor the process more closely. But just what went on down there and how the little creatures managed to make their way to the surface simultaneously was a puzzle. To solve it, the researchers came up with a way to spy on the little guys. They dug out one side of a nest, put in a piece of glass, put a tarp over the hole to keep out light, and took turns crawling into the hole to watch the eggs.

Larry and Harry learned that a turtle that's ready to hatch has an egg tooth sticking up from the nose and uses

This view of hatchling abdomens highlights the differences between the green turtle (left) and a leatherback (right).

it to tear an exit hole in the leathery shell. They observed that when one little turtle cut his way out of the shell and straightened its curled-over body, the movement seemed to stimulate the turtles in nearby eggs to follow suit and tear open their eggs. Soon there were many little turtles stretching their legs, straightening their shells, and generally squirming around and getting in each other's way. As the upper-level hatchlings squirmed and clawed, they disturbed the layer of sand over them, causing the grains to come loose and fall away. As more and more turtles wiggled around, the sand slid around them, migrating toward the bottom of the nest and gradually raising the level of the nest cavity. As more and more sand slipped from overhead to underneath, it lifted the hatchlings toward the surface. Of course the minutes-old hatchlings are not making a conscious effort to get out of the nest. They are just squirming. But when their activity has raised the "floor" beneath them to surface level, almost everyone scrambles out and heads for the sea. Occasionally one or two healthy turtles in a clutch hatch late, only to die in the sand because they missed the chain reaction triggered by the squirming bodies of their siblings.

The Pull of the Sea

Archie Carr had wondered from the outset how the hatchlings know where the sea is. In the dark of night, the tiny creatures always hurried off in the right direction, detouring around beach debris and scrambling over piled-up sand in their race to the water. Instinct told them where they were meant to go, and the ones that didn't get scooped up by predators on shore plunged into the waves to try to outmaneuver the waiting marine predators.

We now know that hatchlings are attracted to the brighter glow of the night sky over the sea, and that the sound and vibration of the surf also help guide them. Today we also know that brightly lit beachfront homes, businesses, and parking lots can override these subtle natural cues and draw hatchlings to their death in swimming pools, parking lots, or under the wheels of traffic. But arriving at that understanding was not a simple process.

Larry Ogren's mission at the Tortuguero station included making behavioral observations and conducting a number of experiments in an effort to find the answers to any number of puzzles. In one early experiment he and Dr. Carr took a batch of hatchling turtles from Tortuguero to San José. From there they caught a ride to Parrita, on the Pacific coast, on a cargo plane loaded with tubular fish traps. Larry and Archie traveled cowboy style astride the fish traps. They wanted to try to determine whether the little turtles were programmed to respond to the magnetic pull of the earth.

Tortuguero's hatchlings always went east, into the sea. If they were guided by the earth's magnetic pull, then they should always travel east. To test this hypothesis, Larry and Archie released the hatchlings on the beach at Parrita: Would they go east toward the mountains, rather than to the sea, in the opposite direction? They soon had their answer, as the little turtles marched westward across the beach and into the Pacific. Apparently the earth's magnetic field wasn't pulling them east. Their instructions had to be coming from another source.

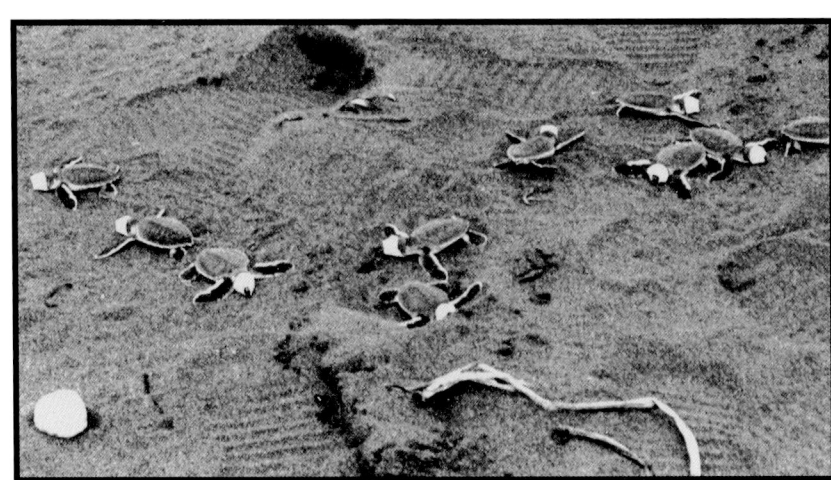

These just hatched turtles wandered aimlessly when their eyes were covered with tape—proving that vision was important in finding their way to the sea.

Finding Facts

Turtles in Spectacles

Imagine if you can, giant turtles strolling the beach wearing eyeglasses. In the 1960s, in a further attempt to unravel the mystery of how turtles find the sea and how they perceive their environment, one of Dr. Carr's former students fashioned eyeglasses with changeable lenses for use on adult turtles. The lenses Dr. David Ehrenfeld used were designed to let in light of certain wavelengths only. To determine how turtles respond to various light waves of various lengths, Ehrenfeld put the glasses on females that were returning to the sea after laying their eggs. He learned that unlike humans, turtles can see ultraviolet light. He also found that they see best in the ultraviolet-to-green region of the spectrum; very little at the red end is visible to them.

In the 1940s a German scientist determined that honeybees can detect polarized light and use the pattern of polarization in the sky to navigate. Ehrenfeld studied sea turtle vision and light characteristics near the sea to test the theory that the turtles used polarized light to not only find the water, but to navigate thousands of miles of open seas. His experiments showed that turtles cannot see polarized light nor do they use celestial navigation. When their eyes are out of the water sea turtles are near-sighted and cannot see well enough to be guided by the stars.

Ehrenfeld examined various other hypotheses, as well; but the only conclusion validated by all the data was that hatchlings looking for the sea, or females returning to the sea after nesting, head for the brightest light that's low on the horizon. Pieces of the puzzle were not exactly dropping seamlessly into place, but through the process of elimination and an occasional "Aha!" a body of knowledge was built.

Turtle hatchlings head for the water, even when they can't see it. That had been demonstrated. So Larry wondered if vision was crucial to their mission of reaching the sea. Would they still manage if they could not see at all? To find out whether the hatchlings were using obvious visual cues, Larry blindfolded a few with strips of adhesive tape and turned them loose on the beach. He smiles now at his primitive methods, but he learned that turtles that couldn't see, couldn't find the sea. They wandered in circles or stood still. He knew then that even though newly hatched turtles couldn't see the ocean, they were seeing something that led them in the right direction. In Tortuguero Larry dug up nests and reburied the clutches of eggs farther from the water's edge to see whether distance was a factor in the turtles' ability to find the sea. He learned that little turtles born closer to the river than to the sea would head for the river, while turtles born farther inland would become disoriented. In addition, he'd noted that on dark, cloudy nights, hatchlings would wander around in confusion. "Light!" Larry thought. It was well known that the sky is usually brighter over both the sea and the river than over land. Could the slight increase in light intensity be the cue that drew the turtles seaward?

The Missing Year(s)

Even more intriguing—and more difficult to solve—than the mystery of how the hatchlings found the sea was the matter of where they went after their plunge into the waves off Tortuguero beach. All scientists knew was humans didn't see green sea turtles again until they were dinner plate size. Archie initially theorized that when the turtles reappeared, they were about a year old. In the 1950s, we had not yet put a man on the moon, much less developed satellite tracking systems. So how do you follow turtles not much bigger than a fifty cent piece as they travel through the ocean?

Carr suspected that the young turtles spent a period of early growth in the open sea. Like some fish, the turtle's bottom side is light colored and the top is dark. To predators looking up from below, the light-colored plastron blends with the light surface of the water. Looking down from the sky, birds see a dark-colored field, the sea; they are unlikely to notice the dark carapace of the turtles. But even with some camouflage, open water is a dangerous place for a bite-sized turtle. And food for small creatures is not concentrated enough in open water to sustain large populations of growing reptiles. The question loomed: Where do they go, and how do they make their living en route?

One biologist, Jane Frick, proposed a radical approach to finding the answer. In Bermuda, Jane, a strong swimmer, had taken to the water to escort the little turtles as far as possible; she was followed by an assistant in a skiff who took periodic bearings from the shore. The two researchers determined that the turtles swam in a straight line away from the shore. This was useful information because the ability to maintain a straight course suggested the presence of some kind of internal navigation system. Jane, therefore, wanted to use in Tortuguero the technique that had succeeded in Bermuda. Chuck Carr, who worked with her at the research station, remembers that his first challenge was persuading Jane that swimming with the turtles in the treacherous currents and bull-shark-infested waters of Tortuguero was out of the question. They finally agreed to try to track the turtles from a rickety observation tower attached to a small aluminum boat. The night before, they collected about 20 just-emerging hatchlings.

Carr wrote, "To get to sea, Jane and I had to negotiate the nearby river mouth, a dangerous, tormented place during the stormy rainy season, just passed. But, we glided through without mishap...." Once in the open sea they rowed a half-mile along the beach to the research station where Shefton Martinez waited with the bucket of turtles. At a signal from the boat, he released the turtles, which immediately headed for the water.

> But we were not the only observers on that beautiful morning. Somewhere, very, very high in the sky there were frigate birds.... The frigates came from nowhere. From the ionosphere, perhaps. They tumbled out of the sky like black and broken kites, and they descended upon the phalanx of swimming turtles.
>
> There were about six of the long-winged, elegant birds, some with handsome white bibs. Avidly, they plucked the little turtles out of the sea.

> Shocked as I was, I was nonetheless able to perceive that the actual kill was an incongruously delicate act. The bird careens down from the heights, zigging and zagging in a vertical plane, and then, just as it reaches the surface, the plunge is arrested, the head dips, the long beak, with its terminal hook, probes downward like a surgeon with a pair of forceps, and the baby turtle is snatched up, flapping wildly of course. [14]

When the attack was over, only a single hatchling remained, possibly saved because it was very close to the boat. Saddened, the two scientists continued their mission with only one hatchling to track. They followed along as the little turtle continued to swim in a straight line out to sea. The turtle would surface, stick its head up and look around, then dive to a depth of about a meter, swim for about a minute, and resurface. Chuck and Jane had followed the tiny creature for approximately four miles when a frigate bird struck again. Swimming at the surface, the turtle spotted the predator and instinctively made a dive. The bird missed a snack, but it did not give up. The turtle dived deeper and stayed down longer than previously, continuing that pattern for several dives. The bird in the meantime revised its strategy. It dropped to sea level and came streaking up from behind as the turtle surfaced. The two scientists, screaming and waving arms and paddles, were able to make the bird abort the attack.

The hour was late, and with the top of Turtle Mountain—the only navigational connection with the shore—about to drop out of sight, the researchers headed back toward the beach. Despite the horror of watching the frigate birds gobble up their turtles, the day had not been lost. Chuck and Jane had watched in fascination as the little turtle navigated a course straight out into the sea long after it had lost any potential navigational clues from shore. They'd also learned that the turtle instinctively knew to watch the sky for predators and to take evasive action. The frigate bird, on the other hand, had proved itself smarter than the turtle by changing its tactics and approaching low and from the rear.

The tracking venture, though disappointing, was a step toward learning about the missing years. Later, another of Dr. Carr's students, Karen Bjorndal and her husband, Alan Bolten, would discover that little loggerheads spend those gap years—between 7 and 12—in the eastern Atlantic, spending much of their time in convergence zones floating in masses of brown algae. This seaweed, called sargassum, floats in large drifts in the temperate and tropical oceans of the world. The mass of seaweed provides the hatchlings with camouflage, resting places, and an abundance of food. Many tiny animals and larval animals also make their home in the sargassum. The young loggerheads dine on these tidbits, not changing their diet to sea grass until they leave the shelter of the sargassum. We still don't know what tells them it is time to move on.

In the 1950s and 1960s methods were not high tech. Moreover, exhausting, frustrating efforts often produced only disappointment. But even experiments that did not appear to have been productive were building blocks to support the next attempt. Bit by bit, understanding of sea turtles was building.

Turtles breeding on the beach is a rare sight. They prefer the privacy and comfort of the water. Perhaps they didn't notice that the waves were pushing them shoreward.

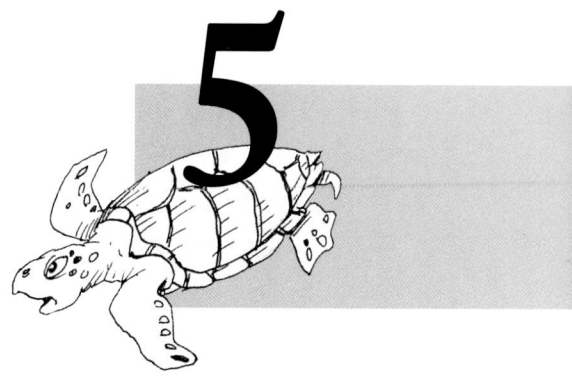

A man rowing a cayuca pauses to take in the phenomena of a U.S. Navy plane floating on the Tortuguero lagoon. The plane would become a familiar sight over a period of almost ten years and its departure with a squirming cargo of thousands of baby turtles would come to seem almost commonplace.

Flying Turtles
And Other Fraught Follies

THE EARLY DAYS of the turtle research station were often marked by frustration, disappointment, and danger; there were acts of heroism, too, sometimes leavened by a touch of humor. These themes are well illustrated by anecdotes that are part of the lore of Tortuguero. They are not stories of failure because each experiment was driven by a passion to know; the aftermath of each narrow escape benefited the turtles or enhanced our knowledge of them. And although results may not have matched anticipations exactly, each contributed to a growing understanding of the world around us. The stories are representative, not unique. They recall a way of life in Tortuguero's John H. Phipps Biological Research Station, and in remote biological field stations around the world.

Larry tends hatchlings in a nest moved to the protected nursery area.

Operation Green Turtle: An Unlikely Coalition

Beginning in 1959, thousands of little green turtles took to the air aboard a U.S. Navy red and white Grumman Albatross amphibious aircraft manned by Navy pilots in orange jumpsuits and biologists in their uniform of sun-bleached, mildew-etched work clothes. The hatchling turtles were on their way to far shores in an attempt to repopulate Caribbean beaches from which the turtles had long since disappeared. Operation Green Turtle (OGT) was a joint venture of the navy and the Tortuguero turtle research station.

The unlikely coalition came about as the result of the navy's interest in the navigational secrets of migrating animals and a little discreet political nudging from a member of the CCC board of directors.

From 1959 until 1968, OGT crews distributed more than 130,000 hatchlings to 28 beaches throughout the greater Caribbean, Mexico, the Bahamas, and even Texas and Florida. It was still a time of turtle slaughter and egg collection on Tortuguero beach, and few hatchlings actually made it to the sea. So the rationale for the project was double edged—to rescue doomed nests and to establish new colonies in places where green turtles had once lived. It was a labor-intensive operation. Freshly laid nests were excavated and the eggs moved to hand-dug nest cavities in a protected area. A wire fence enclosed each nest; the relocated eggs were tended and watched over to preserve them from both human and wild animal predators.

When the hatchlings emerged they were scooped up and transported to wooden troughs protected from the sun by a thatched roof. They were fed on bits of fish, and fresh seawater was brought in daily—one bucketful at a time in the beginning. Later there was a pump for pulling water directly from the sea to the troughs. Sometimes it worked. Transport called for special boxes, which were built from supplies shipped in from Limón. The wooden boxes were about a yard square and a few inches deep. They were lined with plastic and had an absorbent mat to retain moisture during transport. Each housed approximately 200 hatchlings in economy-class comfort.

OGT: Knowing the Way

Dr. Carr supposed from early research that turtles returned to their natal beach to lay their eggs. How they knew where to go was still a mystery. The biologist hypothesized that the key to the turtles' return was somehow implanted in their tiny brains during their trek across the beach and into the sea. Initially some attempts were made to tag the hatchlings

Keeping the cantankerous pump operating and tending the babies prior to shipment was a labor-intensive operation for Larry and Harry.

so they could be recognized when and if they reappeared. But how could the biologists tag an animal that lived in saltwater and would increase in size from a few ounces to hundreds of pounds before it returned to the beach to nest? The tags used on adult turtles would interfere with the hatchling's ability to swim. Pediatric-sized tags, sure to be lost or buried in flesh as the turtle grew, wouldn't have enough room for identifying information anyway.

Larry's attempt to put identifying tags on hatchlings would prove to be wasted effort.

Even so, Larry Ogren experimented with tagging hatchlings. The tags wouldn't survive long, but if young turtles were found or caught in a net with the tags still in place, researchers would have valuable information about the juvenile years. Help seemed to be at hand when fellow biologists engaged in a shrimp-tagging project offered to send Larry some of their small shrimp tags, which he laboriously attached. Getting the tags on was really hard, Larry says—the squirmy hatchlings were not at all in favor of having a plastic disc pinned to their rear flippers. He persevered, however. The plan was that any tags recovered would be sent back to the shrimp taggers and the information forwarded to Tortuguero. Larry waited, hoping for results to start coming in. Nothing. Finally the truth came out: the shrimp taggers had not thought to keep a record of the tag numbers they sent to Larry. If a tag was returned, it was recorded as just another shrimp.

OGT: Lessons learned

Carr and his students understood that their efforts were hampered by their lack of insight into the life of a sea turtle, but the need to do something was urgent. It came down to a hard decision: to take action without benefit of conclusive research data or to postpone action while trying to learn more as the species slipped ever closer to extinction. Carr decided to save as many hatchlings as he could and hope to give them a start in a new location. Sea turtles held in captivity sometimes reached sexual maturity in 6 years, so he anticipated that results from the OGT transplanting efforts would be apparent in 6 or 7 years. Later research, however, showed that in the wild sea turtles don't reach sexual maturity until much later—as long as 30 or 35 years later. So in reality, the earliest results,

Always willing to help, Billy Cruz (right) assists a navy crew member in preparing boxes of turtles for loading.

if they came at all, would be in the 1990s. Dr. Archie Carr died in 1987, and the 1990s came and went while the Caribbean beaches that hosted the transplanted hatchlings remained empty of turtle nests.

In spite of the disappointing outcome, Operation Green Turtle was not a complete failure. Lessons learned in the process added substantially to the growing body of knowledge of the life history of sea turtles. For example, Larry and Leo Martinez observed that when the little turtles were put in the trough, they began a period of frenzied swimming that lasted about a day. That discovery prompted them to recall that hatchlings plunging into the sea react the same way. That initial burst of energy drives them beyond the inshore predators and sets them on their way to the safety and food resources of the sargassum beds, where they pass the first several years of their lives. The turtles in the experiment, however, had already spent that energy frantically swimming around in the troughs, perhaps with disastrous effects on their chances of survival later, when they were released on the beach.

Hatchling turtles were released on beaches around the Caribbean in hopes that they would be imprinted with the location and return there to nest.

To restore the advantage, Carr initiated a smaller project in which the researchers transported not hatchlings but eggs, which were buried on the new home beach. The researchers had been successfully moving eggs from fresh nests to the protected nursery area, where the hatchlings for Operation Green Turtle were raised, but packing the eggs in boxes to be transported by air took more expertise than was available at the time. The experience, however, was useful in that it resulted in a way to move eggs without interrupting their development. Today, every effort is made to protect nests in the location that the female turtle chose, but when there is little likelihood of survival, eggs can be successfully relocated.

OGT: Benefits of the program

The most valuable contributions of Operation Green Turtle fall into the categories of public relations and education. The novel operation brought international media attention to the plight of sea turtles and the heretofore unsung attempts to save them from extinction. The operation was an important part of the growing awareness that taught people to care and to take action. Today many nesting beaches around the world have volunteer groups who walk the beach at all hours and in all kinds of weather. They monitor and protect nesting turtles and the nests they leave behind. Volunteers are on hand at hatchings to protect the little turtles and escort them to the sea, through the gauntlet of predators. The volunteers share turtle lore with bystanders who gather to watch, and they ring doorbells to educate beach residents. As a result, the owners of homes, businesses, and condominiums on many beaches have taken up the cause and switched to special lighting to avoid drawing hatchlings to their deaths in swimming pools and roadways.

Operation Green Turtle also solidified bonds of friendship between the United States and a number of Caribbean countries. The demonstration that the United States cared enough to send naval planes and personnel to remote beaches to attempt to reestablish turtle colonies made a strong and lasting impression on our neighbors to the south. Carr hoped not only to protect marine turtles from extinction, but to reestablish them as a sustainable food source.

As a side benefit, the unusual operation promoted lasting friendships among the navy personnel and the Tortuguero biologists, and spawned good stories that are still shared.

Archie Carr (far left) with one of the US Navy flight crews.

Larry Ogren tells about a harrowing trip over Mexico in a thunderstorm. The load of crew, wooden crates, and turtles was heavy. To minimize weight on takeoff, the OGT planes routinely began their journey only partially fueled and made a stop to top off the tanks. On this trip the crew had made arrangements for a fuel stop in Belize. A promise to have airport personnel meet the Grumman there after hours notwithstanding, the airport was dark and the radios silent. The aircraft was low on fuel, but the pilot, Commander Raymond Curry, decided they could make it to their destination of Mérida, on Mexico's Yucatán Peninsula.

The weather turned bad, however, and storms forced them to fly through heavy rain in a zigzag pattern. Soon they were lost, so Commander Curry dropped lower and lower, looking for landmarks. Then he ordered the crew to rig for a potentially disastrous water landing. As they neared the Gulf of Mexico, they spotted the headlights of a truck that was likely en route, via the new coastal highway, to or from the airport. Given the fifty-fifty chance of being led in the right direction, they followed the truck. Soon they realized, with great relief, that they were nearing the airport. The crew on duty in the tower spoke only Spanish and the crew on the plane spoke only English, but with the gas gauge reading "empty," the Grumman had to land. As they made their approach and touched down on the only runway they could see, a commercial plane came roaring in over their heads. The tension was palpable as the two aircraft barely avoided colliding on the same runway. But the pilot made a safe landing, and their living cargo was delivered to a nearby beach.

On another occasion, an oil leak delayed the Grumman's start on the return trip to Tortuguero. This was not ideal because it meant a tricky nighttime landing on the surface of the lagoon. The less experienced copilot, intending to help, flicked on the plane's lights as they made their approach. The act, of course, was like shining a light on a mirror. The water reflected the harsh light right into the cockpit, temporarily blinding the pilots. The lights were quickly doused, and Commander Curry made a dramatic starlight landing on the Tortuguero lagoon.

Cmdr Raymond Curry was popular with the local children. Here he allows them to examine a hatchling.

OGT: The Lighter Side

Many of the stories were on the lighter side. Larry chuckles gleefully when describing an overnight stop at a U.S. Air Force base in Panama. He joined the crew for a beer in the officers' club, where the men chatted with some air force officers who were curious about this mixed bag of navy officers and civilians in the club. When asked about their mission, Larry responded succinctly, "Operation Green Turtle." One officer quickly said, "Enough said. We don't have a 'need to know.'" Then he added, "But I hope you get that son of a bitch Russian submarine out of there." Larry just smiled. Quick to steer the conversation away from what they thought to be a top-secret topic, the air force personnel offered a story of their own. Fidel Castro was sending planeloads of pencils imprinted with "Viva Castro! Viva Cuba!" to be distributed to Caribbean schools. Offended by this propaganda, the United States responded in kind, and the air force crew had just returned from a pencil mission. Larry asked what our pencils said and, with a straight face, the officer replied, "Dixon No. 2 Soft."

On one occasion, Larry Ogren and Harry Hirth were escorting turtles to the University of Florida in Gainesville. Rather than packing their cargo in sturdy wooden boxes, they were using cardboard containers designed to transport baby chicks. The itinerary, which had begun with a flight to Miami, was about to conclude aboard a train bound for Gainesville. The cardboard turtle boxes were carefully stacked in the back section of the car, along with passenger luggage. It had been a tiring trip, and the two biologists were relaxing and enjoying the comfort of the passenger car when a conductor tapped Larry on the shoulder and asked, "Do you know anything about the little turtles running all over the place?" Larry and Harry spent the rest of the journey chasing turtles around suitcases and down the passenger aisle, and scooping them out from between their fellow passengers' feet.

Beaches Breathe

All the while the turtle guys were digging eggs, tending to a nursery of baby turtles, and building travel crates, they were continuing their tagging and research programs. And when the turtle express came to an end, the work went on at the turtle station. The more they learned, the more they understood that there were secrets just beyond their reach. For example, it made sense for a turtle to bury her clutch of eggs deep in the sand—it gave the developing embryos a more stable temperature and some protection from predators. But they knew that the creatures growing inside the eggshells were somehow absorbing oxygen and emitting carbon dioxide. Where were they getting the oxygen, and why didn't CO2 build up in the nest and poison the entire clutch?

As years passed, new technology made it possible to study the rate of gas exchange in the eggs. Ralph Ackerman, a

The life of hatchiing turtles—before and after they scrabble out of the nest—was cause for much speculation and study by the Tortuguero biologists.

University of Florida graduate student working in the lab and on the beaches of Florida and Tortuguero, devised a method for measuring both oxygen and carbon dioxide in the egg cavities. He found that oxygen levels were higher and carbon dioxide lower than he expected. In 2003 Paul Sotherland, a professor at Kalamazoo College in Michigan, was working with Ackerman and James Spotila at Las Baulas Park on the Pacific coast of Costa Rica. Spotila tells Paul's story in his book *Saving Sea Turtles*.

Paul Sotherland had a theory that the water table below the sand went up and down with the tide. He hypothesized that the tide worked like a bellows, pushing air up and down in the sand, thereby evacuating the CO_2 from the nests and flushing them with fresh oxygen. To check his theory, Paul used a method as basic as those used in the early days at Tortuguero: alone on the beach, he dug a hole. When Paul was long overdue at the camp, the rest of the team went looking for him. They found their colleague on the beach, standing in a hole as deep as he was tall. The sides of the hole had caved in, thanks to Paul's attempts to dig himself out; now the young biologist was trapped in sand that rose higher than his knees.

The next day Paul started over with the aid of a couple of

> ### Murder on the Beach
>
> In June 2013, masked men abducted Jairo Mora Sandoval, a young sea turtle conservationist, and four volunteers. The group had been patrolling the beach at Moín, Costa Rica, to protect leatherback nests from poachers. The volunteers, three from the United States and one from Spain, were left in an abandoned building without shoes or cell phones. In an odd show of consideration, when Grace, a volunteer from the United States, asked for her SIM card back, one of the kidnappers removed it from her phone and returned it.
>
> The volunteers later managed to escape and go for help. But it came too late for Jairo, who evidently was the target of the attack. His body was found on the beach. Investigators first told the press that the cause of death was a gunshot to the head, but Grace said that later reports stated that the young man died of head injuries from a beating. In a newspaper article less than a month earlier, Jairo had proposed that there was a connection between turtle egg poaching, drug trafficking, and organized crime. Jairo Mora was a dedicated conservationist whose death represents a great loss to Costa Rica's environmental programs.

student assistants and an escape ladder. They dug a hole much broader at the top, and terraced, so that the sides couldn't fall in on the diggers. The ladder allowed them to climb out without causing a cave-in—which was a very good thing, since they were 10 feet down when they hit water. Paul inserted a length of large-diameter PVC pipe into the water at the bottom of the hole, which he then backfilled. He attached a rod to a toilet ball float and put it in the pipe. The float rose and fell with the tide. Students sat by the pipe and recorded the level hourly. As the tide rose, air was pushed up through the nests, providing oxygen and flushing away carbon dioxide. Of course, in the early days at Tortuguero, even simple supplies like PVC pipe and a toilet bowl float would have required advance planning to order them from Limón and be sure someone was on hand to take delivery.

Running with Harse

There is an oft-told story of Chuck Carr as a young man racing down the beach on a horse at full gallop, stopping only to flip turtles lying helpless on their backs, awaiting the return of machete-wielding poachers. When asked about the incident, Chuck's mouth twitched up in the wry smile that makes him look a little shy and maybe a bit embarrassed. He said that the story had been somewhat embellished over the years. He did have a horse with him. It was Leo's old horse Harse, and it was more a matter of dragging Harse along behind him as he ran down the beach. It was true, though, that he was flipping turtles, to give them a chance to make it back to the sea before dawn, when the poachers would be back to harvest the valuable calipee.

Like the veladors of old, the poachers turned turtles as they came ashore to nest. The next day, however, rather than facilitating the short trip from the beach to the Bessie, the poachers slaughtered the turtles on the spot. The activity was now illegal, so the poachers worked in haste, taking only the easy-to-carry, easy-to-market calipee, leaving the turtles to die on the beach and their meat to go to waste. Chuck doesn't remember exactly how old he was on that heroic night, but says he must have been really young to be that stupid. The machetes the poachers carried were long and sharp, and the outlaws were intent on protecting their precious illegal harvest. The Black Panther, the leader of the poachers Chuck was outrunning, was known for his cruelty. According to Larry Ogren, he put out the word that he would kill that Carr boy if he showed up in Limón.

Best-laid Plans

Archie Carr as a naturalist resisted the trend toward molecular biology and high-tech science. Yet when technologies were developed that could help him learn about sea turtles, he welcomed the opportunity. Therefore, he was greatly excited when he was granted an electronic address on the Nimbus II satellite, which was launched in May of 1966. The satellite would be able to accurately track a sea turtle on its travels through the seas! Through his tag-and-recapture programs at Tortuguero and other sites, Archie had learned that the old fishermen were right—turtles did travel great distances and return to the same beaches to nest. Tortuguero turtles often showed up in the sea grass beds of Nicaragua several hundred miles away, and tagged turtles returned to Tortuguero to nest after two or three years' absence.

Turtles that nested on the beaches of Ascension Island in the South Atlantic traveled to feeding grounds off the coast of Brazil—a distance of 1,400 miles—and back to Ascension when they felt the urge to reproduce. Ascension Island is a 7-mile-long strip of volcanic rock about midway between Africa and Brazil; there are no landmarks between the two points—only open sea. Even mariners equipped with the most sophisticated equipment available had trouble finding the tiny island. For a turtle, the feat of navigation was stunning, and biologists hungered to know how they accomplished it.

Dr. Carr dreamed of all the great data that would be collected by the satellite, while consultants designed a radio transmitter that the chosen turtle would drag behind as she traveled. An amazing device was completed and delivered to Archie. The tubular metallic machine had an antenna, a lead keel, and a propeller that would record the turtle's speed through the water. The equipment would transmit data, including the exact location of the turtle, to the Nimbus satellite, which would transmit it to a station in the United States. Archie made the long flight on an air force cargo plane to Ascension Island, where he supervised the attachment of this custom-built device to the shell of a nesting turtle. Carr believed that the satellite information would provide insight into the turtle's route and navigation methods as she made her way to Brazil or to some other destination they did not yet know about.

In an article for *Conservation Biology*, Chuck Carr wrote about the excitement in the Carr household before the trip and the family's anticipation as they waited two weeks for the traveler's return. The children questioned their father eagerly, and learned that Ascension Island was remarkable and that the turtles were larger than those of Tortuguero—many weighed as much as 500 pounds. Chuck wrote:

> But Daddy, Daddy, what about the transmitter?" we cried. "What about Nimbus II?" Mother gazed at him, alarm growing in her knowing eyes. "The radio flooded," Daddy said with disgust. "We wired it to the turtle. She walked off the beach into the sea and the radio filled with water. It cracked and popped. The radio was not waterproof. They forgot to make it water proof!"[15]

Technology has changed, but the need to know has not, and as Archie Carr learned on Ascension Island, even high-tech methods can—and often do—go wrong. Biologists are still driven by a passion to understand what makes the planet tick. And the importance of understanding the intricately woven web of life on earth is becoming more evident every day as we face climatic changes and an unprecedented number of extinctions.

6

In 1998 Leo Martinez celebrated his 80th birthday. Larry was working on a leatherback project in Parismina at the time and made a trip to Tortuguero to wish his old friend a happy day. Two years later, unable to be in Tortuguero to celebrate with Leo, Larry sent him this photo framed with the message below.

*To Leo Martinez
In Celebration of Your 82nd Birthday
My Unforgettable Compadre Who Shared His Ranch
And So Much More With Me in Those Early Years
My Warmest Greetings to You.
Larry Ogren*

And Life Goes On

IT HAS BEEN almost 60 years since Archie Carr started the world's first sea turtle research and tagging program in Tortuguero. Larry Ogren, Harry Hirth, and the other early researchers were called "marooners" because of their isolation from the world. But although they lacked what most of us consider the most basic of necessities, they adapted. They depended on the local people for friendship, food, and guidance. They learned to improvise and do without, and they devised simple methods to learn complex truths about turtles. The hardship they endured and the ingenuity it spawned followed them through life; their work is the foundation of turtle biology and of conservation biology, as well.

Larry Ogren maintained an association with the CCC/STC throughout his career. He returned to Costa Rica often to assist with various projects and even now is an emeritus member of the STC board of directors. Larry's life path was set in Tortuguero. He devoted his career to the protection and conservation of marine turtles. In Florida, as the specialist in endangered sea turtles at the National Marine Fisheries Service, he reviewed research showing a direct correlation between the opening of shrimping season and the number of dead turtles washing up on the shore. To reduce this mortality, he searched for a method to protect turtles from shrimp trawls—a method that would have minimal impact on the harvest.

Trawls are nets that are pulled behind a boat, or two boats working together. When the nets are deployed, air-breathing turtles get caught in the mesh and drown. TEDs (turtle excluder devices) are devices that allow turtles to swim out of the nets while keeping most of the shrimp inside. Different models have been tried, but all allow some of the shrimp catch to escape along with the turtles and other bycatch, a result that made shrimpers reluctant to use the excluders.

Larry donned scuba gear and followed shrimp trawls to watch the behavior of turtles when the nets approached. Perhaps the correlation reported between turtle deaths and the start of shrimping season was a coincidence. Perhaps the TEDs could be modified in a way that hadn't been tried yet, a way that would keep all the shrimp in the net.

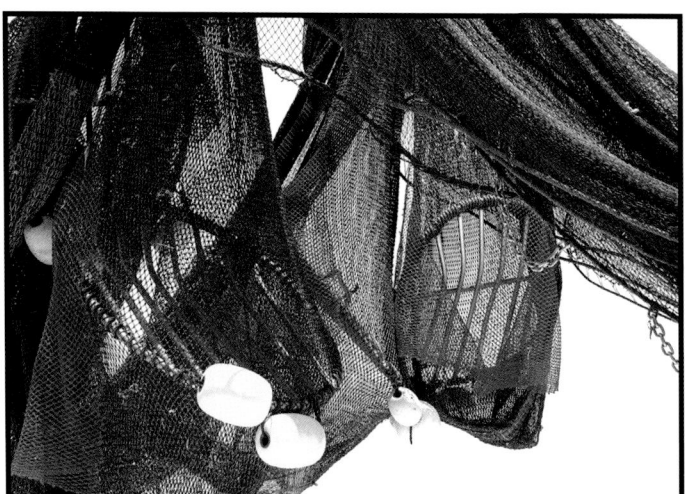

TEDs attached to shrimp nets allow shrimp to be netted while preventing turtles and other large marine life from getting swept into the trawls.

The turtles, Larry found, were leery of the big nets and tried to stay ahead of them; when they tired, however, they slowed down and soon became entangled. Larry, working with the Gear Research Team from the Pascagoula, Mississippi NMFS lab, studied trawls fitted with different types of TEDs, hoping to identify the devices that were most effective for the shrimpers and least harmful to the turtles. Bolstered by his underwater research, Larry fought for the mandatory installation of the devices on shrimp trawls.

Most shrimpers, however, were very much against any measure that would force them to acquire and use TEDs. Thus the devices, meant to be a compromise to allow both shrimpers and turtles to survive, were instead a source of bitter controversy and rebellion. The fight was long and heated, but in 1987, the Florida legislature passed a law requiring all trawling shrimp boats to equip their nets with TEDs. Two years later, Congress enacted the Shrimp-Turtle Law, which requires all countries that export shrimp to the United States to certify that only boats equipped with TEDs had harvested the catch.

Larry, who never misses an opportunity to find a note of humor, even macabre humor, tells a story of a demonstration by shrimpers to protest the new legislation. During a Florida Marine Fisheries Commission meeting in Tallahassee, shrimpers and their supporters were gathered in front of the capitol building with signs proclaiming "STOP TED." They were soon confronted by an opposing group bearing "SAVE TED" signs. It seems the second group thought the shrimpers' signs referred to the impending execution of Ted Bundy, the serial killer. Knowing nothing of shrimp or turtles, they'd assumed that the trawlers were supporters of the death penalty and hastily made signs of their own to protest the "TED" protesters. Both groups were unsuccessful.

Other Tortuguero Veterans

Archie Carr not only passed on his passion to his students but taught them, through his own writing, the importance of being able to write and speak clearly and simply about complex subjects. The names of many of the Tortuguero veterans have become legendary in the annals of marine turtle biology and conservation biology. Harry Hirth is a professor emeritus of biology at the University of Utah. David Ehrenfeld, a professor of biology at Rutgers University and the first editor of the journal of *Conservation Biology,* is the author of several popular books. James Spotila's books include *Sea Turtle* a beautiful full-color volume on the biology, behavior, and conservation of sea turtles, as well as *Saving Sea Turtles*, a good read on the biologists and processes of sea turtle biology that have contributed to our understanding.

In the mid-1970s, researchers learned that the sex of certain species of freshwater turtles was determined by the temperature in their nests. Spotila and another biologist, Ed Standora, were curious to know if the same thing occurred in marine turtles. Invited by Carr to come to Tortuguero to study the matter, they recruited David Ehrenfeld; soon the three had put together a team of research assistants.

The project was well timed, for until very recently, measuring the temperature in a well-buried sea turtle nest had been impossible. Spotila, Standoro, and Ehrenfeld, however, were able to use a new thermocouple device to capture accurate measurements of the temperature in a nest. The team discovered that during a certain period of sea turtle embryo development, temperature is indeed the factor that determines sex in the hatchlings. Specifically, cooler temperatures produce males and warmer temperatures produce females.

Archie's Angels

The last three graduate students Carr accepted, all female, came to be known as Archie's Angels. Larry says, "Carr loved those gals. They were dedicated scientists, who went to any lengths to accomplish their goals, they caused no problems,

Karen Bjorndal checks a nesting turtle.

and they kept good field notes, and even more importantly, wrote and published papers on their work." All three are now among the leading sea turtle biologists in the world.

The first of the trio to study with Carr as a postgrad was Karen Bjorndal, who is now the director of the Archie Carr Center for Sea Turtle Research at the University of Florida. Recognized today as the world's leading expert on Chelonia mydas, the green sea turtle, as Archie's student she studied the animal's diet and digestive processes. She put diapers on captive turtles so she could poke through their poop to find out what it contained and how well that food had been processed. After learning that in the Caribbean Chelonia's diet consisted almost exclusively of sea grass, she studied grass beds. Dr. Bjorndal was the first to note that green turtles have a marked effect on sea grass beds, and she was quick to point out that their extinction could change the ecology of tropical seas.

Anne and Peter Meylan, both turtle biologists, work together to weigh a turtle.

Another angel was Anne Meylan, who did her doctoral thesis on the feeding ecology of hawksbill turtles. She learned that adult hawksbills dine almost exclusively on sponges. But the startling discovery was that they show a preference for species that contain needlelike silica spines, called spicules, which can puncture or lodge in the hawksbill's internal organs; these sponges also produce toxic chemicals. To build up a tolerance to the sharp spikes and the toxins, the juvenile hawksbill changes its diet gradually, to condition its digestive system to accept the noxious materials. No one knows why the turtles undergo this difficult process, but biologists note that the silica-bearing sponges are a food source for which there is very little competition.

The discovery that hawksbills eat glass cost Anne a hand. While she was examining the stomach contents of a hawksbill, some of the silica spicules stuck in her right hand and broke off beneath the skin. Years later a tumor formed around a shard in one finger and spread to her right hand, which had to be removed; but her energy and dedication to her work were unscathed. Dr. Meylan is a senior research scientist with the Florida Fish and Wildllife Conservation Commission in St. Petersburg

The third angel, Jeanne Mortimer, has studied sea turtles in some 20 countries with emphasis on the Seychelles, an island group in the Indian Ocean; she has written extensively for both adults and children. Jeanne scored a spectacular success for the turtles when she took on the U.S. Air Force to protect a nesting beach. She'd learned that the military was about to build a new runway on Ascension Island and wanted to source the concrete aggregate locally. The plan was to remove sand—tons of it—from an important nesting beach. Jeanne took her concerns straight to top brass in Washington and, as a result, the contractors were instructed to find their aggregate elsewhere.

Like Anne Meylan, Jeanne has also taken a special interest in hawksbills—one of the most seriously endangered sea turtles. Dr. Mortimer, who chairs the Hawksbill Task Force for the International Union for Conservation of Nature (IUCN) Marine Turtle Specialist Group, often speaks out on the subject. She says "Of all the species of sea turtles, the hawksbill has experienced the longest and most sustained history of commercial exploitation. Primarily as a result of this trade, hawksbills have declined by 80 percent or more during the last three hawksbill generations throughout their global range."[17] The exploitation here is not primarily for meat and eggs, though eggs are often taken, but for the hawksbills' beautiful translucent shells.

Coconuts Falling Near the Tree

And of course, there were the Carr offspring. With both parents celebrated conservationists, Archie and Marjorie's children acquired a reverence for the world around them. They all visited Tortuguero as youngsters and as teenagers, and each of the four boys spent at least a season or two working the turtle beach. Mimi, the oldest of the Carr flock, became an actress. She has expressed her love of nature and her family heritage through videos such as *Celebrating a Forgotten Place: The Carr Family Cabin in the Florida Scrub.*

Chuck, David and Tom Carr. Life choices for all of the Carr children reflect their parents dedication to conservation biology.

Chuck, as senior conservationist with the Wildlife Conservation Society, was in charge of the group's projects in Central America. Now retired, he serves on the board of directors of the Sea Turtle Conservancy, farms a portion of the family land near Gainesville, and keeps bees for delicious wildflower honey. He is also a talented writer and has contributed generously to this book.

Steve spent numerous seasons studying Gulf sturgeon on the Suwannee River. The task entailed netting the big fish, then measuring, tagging, and releasing them in a procedure similar to that used in the turtle work.

Tom was described by David Ehrenfeld as one of the best naturalists he had ever known—possibly even better than Archie. Tom, always something of an adventurer, has channeled his appreciation for nature into designing educational, ecosensitive tours to wilderness areas all over the world. Larry Ogren has very fond memories of a rafting trip down the Rio Plátano in Honduras with Tom as his guide. With a chuckle, Tom recalls that they started the trip on muleback. Larry was a little hesitant about riding a mule, so Tom made sure he was given a docile one. Her name was Muñeca, which means "doll" in Spanish. Larry grew fond of Muñeca and was afraid she would get lost trying to find her way home after he and Tom had left the mules to continue their journey by raft—he wanted to share his raft with her. The mule, however, made its own way safely home.

David, the youngest son, worked at Florida Defenders of the Environment and the Caribbean Conservation Corporation and served on the staff of the Agriculture and Natural Resources subcommittee of the Florida House of Representatives. David and his wife, Peggy, a University of Florida professor, bought a property near Gainesville that was threatened by development. On the outskirts of the picturesque little town of Micanopy, they renovated the old gas station as Pearl's Country Store and Barbecue, now a highly rated restaurant and catering service.

Over lunch in January, 2013. Larry and Tom reminisce with much laughter and camaraderie

Tom Carr died in November 2013.

Following Tom's death, his brother, Chuck, told Larry, "You were always his hero." Larry says, "I didn't know how to respond to that, because Tom was my hero. He was such a free spirit. Always ready for an adventure."

While working for NMFS, because of Tom's fluency in Spanish, Larry was often able to employ him as an interpreter for field trips and aerial surveys of nesting beaches. In 1978 they went to Rancho Nueva, Mexico just prior to the annual Kemps ridley arribada as an advance team to check nesting conditions and local reactions. By day they posed as entrepreneurs looking for a site to open a fishing lodge. By night they coaxed an old VW beetle into areas where outsiders were not welcome and where most 4WD vehicles would have difficulty.

Upgrades and Modernization

David Godfrey came to work for CCC (now STC) in 1993 having spent the previous five years working for Marjorie Carr. In 1997, a few days before his 30th birthday, he was appointed executive director and holds that position today. As a birthday gift, Archie's widow had a courier deliver a note and a package; the note said that Archie would have been proud to have David as a part of CCC. The package contained a pre-Columbian carved stone sea turtle that had been Archie's. Marjorie Carr, who clearly expected great things from her protégé, would not be disappointed if she were alive today to savor his accomplishments.

Godfrey guides the international organization through the hurdles of fundraising, strategic planning, and managing staff, as well as communicating the message of sea turtle conservation to the media, the public, and elected officials. He identifies threats to marine turtles and their habitats, seeks solutions to these threats, and campaigns to bring about policy changes that address the problems. An energetic, personable organizer, he surrounds himself with dedicated staff who share his passion for their mission. Under his directorship, not only has Tortuguero's John H. Phipps Biological Field Station expanded and modernized, but the STC has established a variety of programs in the United States and Panama. The organization is an international leader in establishing policy and fighting to save marine turtles from extinction.

Larry Ogren says that one of the good staffing decisions Godfrey made was to hire Sebastian Troeng as the station's scientific director. Between 1997 and 2006, Sebastian reorganized, updated, and improved research, data collection, and recording techniques. Dr. Troeng is currently a senior vice president with Conservation International.

Larry first met Sebastian Troeng when the new scientific director called him for advice. Jaguars had been killing turtles and leaving the corpses behind on the beach. Sebastian had

Since the early days in Leo's house, the Tortuguero marooners have enjoyed three homes.

Top: The house designed by Carr and built on Leo's property. The stilt structure, built on a concrete slab, was an innovation for Tortuguero. It lifted the living area up to catch the sea breezes and provided covered storage and work space below. Leo collected many loads of rock and gravel in his cayuca to construct the concrete slab.

Middle: Casa Verde, remembered fondly by many Tortuguero veterans.

Bottom: The concrete block structure which replaced Casa Verde, provides both housing and workspace for modern marooners.

been gathering and burying the victims, but the next morning there would be more. Knowing that jaguars like their meat aged, Larry suggested leaving the dead turtles on the beach. He explained that the predators had been killing turtles, eating a few choice parts, and abandoning the rest to allow it to ripen. But when they came back the next night and found that their stash had mysteriously disappeared, they simply killed more turtles.

By the late twentieth century, jaguars had almost disappeared in Costa Rica, but thanks to the country's aggressive conservation programs their numbers now are growing. Jaguars still prey on turtles, but natural predation is sustainable, while exploitation is not. In an interview published online, Julienne Gage emphasizes this point by quoting Dr. Troeng: "Never before has there been the level of global awareness of the need for a healthy planet to ensure human well-being and survival that there is today. . . . Fortunately, because ocean degradation and poor management are caused by humans, it is also within our power to resolve these problems."[16]

Emma Harrison, STC scientific director, and the author (left) in San José, Costa Rica.

What's Happening at the Station?

Key STC personnel in Costa Rica as of 2013 include Costa Rica director, Roxana Silman, and scientific director, Emma Harrison, both based primarily in San José. Field coordinator Catalina González and station manager Randall Torres oversee operations at Tortuguero, and education coordinator Juan Guerrero is in charge of outreach projects.

Field research coordinator Catalina González Prieto explains the nesting data displayed in charts posted in the Phipps station work room.

Argentinian Alan Rosenthal, a research assistant, relaxes with his laptop.

Over the years, the infrastructure has grown and evolved from the earliest accommodations: first Larry's single bunk in the sawmill, then on to a room in the house of Leo Martinez and next, in 1960, to the simple stilt house a village carpenter, Chico Montalbán, built for the researchers on Leo's property. The stilt house was a virtual palace for the marooners.

A few years later, in 1963, Billy Cruz helped the CCC purchase a green wooden building that had been built and briefly used by the United Fruit Company. It came to be known as Casa Verde (green house) and served as home for the station for 30 years. Staff and volunteers struggled to stay ahead of the termites, dampness, and rot that consume wooden

LIFE GOES ON

> ### TAGGING DATA
>
> In 1955, the first year of the tagging program, 644 turtles were turned between July 2 and August 29. Of those, 149 were recaptures, turtles that had been caught and tagged earlier in the season: of the 149, 44 were recaptured twice, 7 three times, and 2 were recaptured 4 times. The recaptures provided the first indication that turtles nest more than once in a season. Recaptures also allow researchers to follow a few turtles over a long period of time. In 2012, 740 previously tagged turtles were recaptured. Of those, 173 had first been tagged more than 10 years earlier, and 10 more than twenty years earlier. The longest recorded nesting history was a turtle last encountered in 2011; she was first tagged in 1980—31 years before.
>
> In 2012, an estimated 172,760 green turtle nests were laid. Considering that most females nest from two to five times in a season, this would suggest a population of between 28,793 and 61,700 nesting females. Evidence of poaching of either eggs or turtles was seen on half of STCs daily surveys. Dogs destroyed nine green turtle nests and a minimum of 69 green turtles were killed by jaguars. STC researchers and volunteers put in more than 2,000 patrol hours between June 6 and October 31. On August 18, 3459 new nests were counted, the largest number for a single night. The number of nests fluctuates from year to year with 78,852 in 2011 and in 2010 180,310 green turtles nested on 18 miles of Tortuguero beach. On a single night, August 28, researchers counted 3,384 nests. The STC annual reports, published on the organization's website, www.conserveturtles.com, give detailed nesting statistics, as well as information on leatherback, loggerhead, and hawksbill nesting activity on Tortuguero beach.

structures in the jungle, but in vain. In 1995, too far gone to salvage, Casa Verde was torn down. Any salvageable materials such as corrugated roof panels, reusable wood, electrical, and plumbing materials were reused or donated to the village.

Today the Phipps Biological Research Station facilities consist of a concrete block dormitory and work building, a dining hall that doubles as a meeting and classroom building, a small museum and gift shop, and a video screening room. There is also a separate dormitory to house volunteers, who pay for the privilege of participating in the strenuous nightly beach walks and other station activities. Those activities now include outreach and education as well as turtle monitoring,

Turning Turtles

Education & Outreach Coordinator Juan Daniel Guerrero Blanco, from Spain talks to a new group of research assistants in the museum.

tagging, and research in both green turtle and leatherback turtle nesting seasons.

The STC employs approximately seven permanent staff in San José and Tortuguero, a dozen or so in the United States, and two in Panama, plus local cooks, building and maintenance personnel, security, and a boat captain. In green turtle season the station recruits research assistants, who in groups of six to eight serve 6-week internships; another smaller group works leatherback season, which occurs earlier in the year than the green turtle nesting. The research assistants still walk the beach in the dark and face the same dangers and frustrations that challenged the first marooners more than half a century ago. Now though, they work a four-hour shift on the darkened beach, either from 8:00 p.m. until midnight or from midnight until 4:00 a.m. And of course, they perform other duties during daylight hours. Techniques have changed somewhat on the beach. Turtles are no longer turned— flipped over onto the back. The researchers decided that making the turtle lie on its back for hours put unnecessary stress on its internal organs—not to mention the indignity of the manhandling. Fortunately, with more people on the beach, the tagging and data collecting can be done on the spot. A hen that is making her nest and laying eggs is focused on the job at hand, in fact in a trancelike state. While she takes care of her business, the research assistants do the same. They affix a tag to her flipper, or if she already bears a tag they record the information. They weigh, measure, check for injuries and tumors, count eggs, and mark the location of the nest so it can be monitored daily. The station now has electricity, running water, and a few window air conditioners. The change from the '50s and '60s is extreme, but the crew still works long hours, and though the isolation is not as absolute, there are still no roads and no cars in Tortuguero. The village has a few cafés, but running into Limón for a beer or to buy a new pair of shoes is not an option.

Where Have the Turtles Been?

Tagging returns, computerized data, and new instrumentation have demonstrated in indelible terms that the uneducated coastal fishermen had informed Archie Carr correctly when he queried them about turtles. They knew, because they knew the sea, that sea turtles traveled the globe and came back to their natal shore to reproduce. The tagging program showed it to be true. But we had to wait by the sea for the tags to come back.

Transmitters are affixed to a turtle's shell in a way that allows maximum service life for the equipment without harming the turtle.

When turtles crawl up on the beach wearing Tortuguero tags, we know they have been there before, and we know whether it was 2 weeks ago or 20 years ago. Tags showing up back at Tortuguero in the years after the inaugural tagging in 1955 proved beyond a shadow of a doubt that turtles return to the same beach. Data gathered on the beach at Tortuguero has provided much information on the turtles' nesting behavior, but one of the earliest questions remains: Where have they been? The all-important answers are provided year after year by tags that are sent back from far places. Unfortunately, a returned tag usually means a dead turtle, one that has been caught in a shrimp

117

net or washed up on a distant beach, where someone has noticed the tag and removed it. All the information from the returned tags, and from the historical record, is used to chart turtle migrations. Tagging data accumulated over decades has demonstrated that sea turtles travel hundreds or thousands of miles between feeding grounds and nesting beaches, even when there are other feeding grounds located much closer to their nesting beach.

New technology retells old stories in more precise scientific terms, showing clearly that sea turtles are global animals. In the old days, the tags showed that turtles consistently returned to the same beach—perhaps, many suspected, the beach where they were hatched. But because hatchling turtles had not been successfully tagged, there was no data to support that supposition. Now detailed migration records have been supplemented by DNA analyses, and individual turtles can be identified with a particular beach. DNA results can also demonstrate that some of the turtles feeding in Nicaragua also nest on Tortuguero beach. Similarly, turtles feeding in Brazil nest on Ascension Island. Not only can we identify turtles by DNA, but Archie Carr's dream of tracking turtles by satellite is now a reality. Scientists can follow a turtle on its travels around the world, and so can you—by going to the STC's website, www.conserveturtles.com, and clicking on "Track a sea turtle."

To allow people to follow a turtle on its travels, researchers

Indira Torrez Ocampos (left), manager of the station gift shop, enjoys browsing old station photos on the author's IPad along with Noel Lau Hernández, a guide (center), and another unidentified guide.

attach a waterproof platform terminal transmitter (PTT) to its back by a method that neither harms the turtle nor interferes with its movements; the expensive tracking devices continue to work for up to a year, then fall off harmlessly. Two methods are used to attach the PTTs to hard-shell turtles, and a third was devised for the soft-shell leatherback.

Tour de Turtles

Each year since 2008, STC has hosted Tour de Turtles, an Internet-based interactive turtle migration marathon. It is a fun and educational way to focus worldwide attention on one central fact: marine turtle survival is a global problem that cannot be resolved without international cooperation—our turtles are your turtles. Tortuguero can't protect its turtles if Nicaraguans dine on turtle soup.

In Tour de Turtles, more than a dozen turtles are fitted with transmitters and followed for three months from their nesting beaches as they travel to their foraging grounds. Each turtle has a page on the Tour de Turtles website, where photos and interactive maps let visitors to the site track its movements. The turtle that travels the farthest in three months is proclaimed the winner. Turtles can also win in the Causes Challenge, so named because each turtle represents a particular threat to sea turtle survival. Fans can donate to their cause and the turtle that raises the most money is declared the winner.

Tour de Turtles is designed to raise awareness of sea turtles and the challenges they face, and the scientific community benefits from the data collected on little-known migration routes. To help school children enjoy the fun of the Tour, a free educators' guide is available for teachers. Only the combined efforts of the world community can ensure the survival of sea turtles. The more we know about where they live and how they make their living—the better their chances of survival.

Eighty-five year old Bill Sambola has seen many changes come to the Bogue. His love and knowledge of his home make him a popular guide.

It's Still Pura Vida in Turtle Bogue

THERE IS A clatter of activity at La Pavona boat launch. Returning tourists grab the hands of grinning guides and jump from open boats, landing with a wet splat on the sand. They watch anxiously for their luggage, which will be tossed from a multicolored pile remaining on their boat or come puttering up in a separate luggage boat. The ever-cheerful guides sort the gaggle of incoming and outgoing tourists and their accoutrements—sending some toward the waiting buses and helping others make the long step from shore to ship.

My friend Mary and I had been picked up from our San José hotel at 6:00 a.m. by a modern bus that belonged to Pachira Lodge. We had managed to hitch a ride to the village of Turtle Bogue because we were booked to spend the last few days of our trip at Evergreen, Pachira's sister lodge. Our guide was already on board, providing a barrage of chatter in alternating English and Spanish, his voice overrode conversations in a variety of languages, creating a pleasant babel. The bus trip from San José had taken approximately five hours, including a stop for breakfast. The journey by boat to Tortuguero would take another hour or two.

I exchanged greetings with Noel, a guide I knew from a previous trip. Instead of squeezing Mary and me onto the crowded Pachira boat, he helped us secure seats on a boat transporting workers to the various lodges, making sure the captain understood that we were to be dropped off at Miss Junie's. We grabbed outside seats near the front on opposite sides of the narrow aisle. I thought wistfully of Larry flying in on the Aerovias Costarricenses Cessna and being paddled down the lagoon by Bertie. But both the airline and Bertie are long gone. Now a small passenger plane makes daily flights from San José to a landing strip where boats wait to motor passengers on to the village or surrounding lodges. The bus/boat trip takes longer, but is fun and less expensive; the lodges include it in their package prices.

Visitors arriving by boat are welcomed by giant sculptures overlooking a pretty park.

Welcome to Turtle Bogue

The village is much changed since Larry Ogren lived there with Leo Martinez and took his meals with Sibella, Leo's sister. Sibella's house is gone and, according to Dorling Taylor, the El Collbri souvenir shop and Buda's Caffe occupy the site of Leo's house. Our boat dropped us on the sandy shore of Miss Junie's property. Her grandson Byron, who'd come down to greet us, dragged our luggage up the steep bank and over to the lodge reception area. After settling in, we wandered into the village and stopped to watch the tourist boats tie up at the small waterfront park in the center of the village, under the watchful gaze of two giant colorful statues. a toucan and a parrot. The unpainted thatch-roofed houses are gone—replaced by concrete block buildings roofed in tin. Paint colors are cheerful and bright, and several buildings are adorned with colorful murals of local wildlife and other subjects. The sea turtle is commemorated in concrete statuary, murals, and mosaics, as well as in knick-knacks and jewelry displayed in the several souvenir shops. There is a school and a grocery, a few restaurants, and basic tourist accommodations. The village now stays in touch with the rest of the world through mail, telephone, and e-mail, but communication can be iffy, depending partly on the weather.

There are no cars or trucks in Tortuguero. Goods brought in from Limón on small boats are moved about the village on handcarts.

Despite the advent of tourism, the village feels authentic. It lacks the slick, plasticized, commercial display of many modern tourist venues. The artwork designed to entice visitors has a primitive charm that suits the setting. The people are open and friendly, and the few restaurants serve up local

dishes, although what is offered does not always jibe with the menu. Shipments from Limón are more reliable now, but as before, much depends on what is available on any given day. Local fish dishes are still popular if someone has caught fish, but the daily fare does not include turtle, manatee, or tepezcuintle!

There are still no roads leading to Tortuguero, though one paved street stretches from near the ranger station at the national park through the village, ending abruptly at Miss Junie's wooden gate, with its hand-carved, wooden sea turtle. Transportation in the village is by foot, boat, or bicycle. Young men with rubber-wheeled pushcarts collect goods from wooden docks, deliver them to waiting merchants, and return with cases of empty beer bottles. Sand paths lead to the school and houses that sit away from the single center street. In the village proper the street no longer meanders around coconut trees. Coconuts still grow on Miss Junie's property, however, and you will do well to stay on the path if it is the season for falling coconuts. There is even an Internet café, though Wi-Fi service is spotty. For tourists, home seems a long way away—another world. Older residents probably share that feeling of disconnect from a familiar lifestyle. For them, changes to the village must seem rapid and radical.

First Family

The history of the Martinez family is the history of Turtle Bogue. Walton Martinez, a ship builder and trader from San Andres, Colombia, knew the Bogue as a place of great numbers of turtles and therefore a place with good prospects for making a living. Economic conditions were changing in Colombia in the early 1920s, and some of Walton's nine children had moved away. The patriarch then determined that it was time to relocate the remaining members of his household. When he decided on the move to Turtle Bogue, he sold his business interests in San Andres and sailed to Tortuguero with Leo, his youngest son, to establish a homestead. There were a few turtle harvesters living there at the time, and Martinez gradually bought their land. Eventually all but two of his children joined him in the Bogue.

Leo's job in the early years was to raise chickens and pigs, as he had done in San Andres. Edna Gail Dases, who interviewed Leo at the turn of the century, quotes his recollections of his youthful responsibilities: "It was my responsibility to walk over to the old volcano, which we now call the cerro, and round up our pigs which freely pastured there.... In those days, there were many tigers [Central American people often refer to jaguars as tigers] living there and they would follow the pigs. It was a hard and dangerous chore."[18]

By the time the turtle station opened, Walton Martinez had died. But Leo and his brothers Sam, Obid, and Shefton worked with the turning and tagging program, while their sister, Sibella, and later her daughter Junie, cooked for the biologists. Miss Junie's cooking is remembered with fondness by the many researchers who have eaten at her table, and the old-timers praise her mother's cuisine, as well.

Taking a break from her busy day, Miss Junie relaxes on a bench outside of her home.

Miss Junie has not given up cooking for hungry gringos. She now owns a hotel and restaurant, and at 75 still does much of the cooking. She is the head of a strong family unit, the next generation of which consists of her children: five daughters, Karol, Noly, Purl, Dorling, and Karla, and her son Cleoid; a daughter, Gloria, is deceased. And then there are grandchildren, siblings, cousins, nieces, and nephews. Miss Junie's property sits between the village and the turtle station, which makes it convenient for her to maintain a warm relationship with the biologists. The hotel is rustic and charming, but a spot on the end balcony gets pretty good Wi-Fi reception. With your back against the upper-level porch railing, you can view the sea to your left and the lagoon to your right while finding a tenuous e-mail connection to your other life.

The station now has its own kitchen. When I visited in August of 2012, Juanita Fernandez and Miss Junie's cousin Eliza Alvin Garcia were cheerfully chopping vegetables for the evening meal. Most of Miss Junie's family members, however, are involved with tourism. The whole family seems to pitch in to help with the lodge and restaurant, with grandson Byron taking a leading role.

Miss Junie's cousin Eliza Alvin Garcia (foreground) carries on the family tradition of cooking for the biologists along with Juanita Fernandez (background).

Dorling owns a bakery in the village, and Noly guides tourists eager to view nesting turtles; Cleoid is a nature guide for one of the nearby lodges, and Karla, a naturalist, operates her own business.

Karla was one of 22 Costa Rican students chosen from among several hundred applicants to be awarded a scholarship by the University of Pennsylvania to study taxonomy. The classes were primarily held on the mountains and in the forests of Costa Rica. After completing the course, Karla accepted a job with the privately funded National Institute of Biodiversity in the western part of the country. For seven years she worked on their initiative to inventory every living species in Costa Rica—a daunting task considering that Costa Rica, though covering only 0.03 percent of the planet's surface, contains 5 percent of the world's biodiversity, a density unmatched anywhere else on earth.

Karla later worked for several tourism companies, but she missed home and wanted to be her own boss. She moved back to Tortuguero and started her own business: Karla Taylor—Travel Advisor. Karla, who offers various travel services, has been described as "[19]a walking encyclopedia of lore about Costa Rica's flora and fauna." She specializes in canoe trips on the rivers and canals. Miss Junie's youngest daughter says the best thing about being a guide is that it allows her to "see the world through other people's eyes."

Karla Taylor, Travel Advisor, chats with the author on the balcony of Miss Junie's lodge.

Bill Sambola, another popular canoe guide and close friend of the Martinez family, was one of the men who paddled up the Agua Fria in the dark to rescue 14-year-old Chuck Carr and biologist Harry Hirth. Mention the incident to Bill today and he slaps his thigh and shouts, "Hah! Chuck!" and laughs long and hard. Bill says he has been "pushing" a canoe through the waters of Tortuguero since the age of 6. As a young man he worked for the turtle station, and at 85 he paddles his canoe with up to four passengers on round-trip explorations lasting 4 hours.

Mary and I joined Bill for a canoe tour. He likes to leave around 5:00 a.m. to beat the other boats to the ranger station, where everyone must pay the $10 park fee. After paying, we headed across the lagoon, threading between boats now waiting their turn to get to the ranger station. On the far side, Bill slipped the canoe into a slough that reached a narrow finger into the dense jungle. As he paddled, he spotted wildlife, identified the flora and fauna of his home, and regaled us with local lore. Back on the shore in front of Miss Junie's, he spent an hour or so calmly wielding a machete to chop away the outer shells of green coconuts, a local skill that has you holding your breath as the blade descends toward each coconut, held in the machete expert's unprotected hand. Mary and I hung around to watch him work, and he paused to whack off the top of three of the denuded coconuts, creating a "pipa" of refreshing coconut water each for Mary, me, and Karla's young son. Before heading home, Bill loaded his canoe with scraps from Miss Junie's restaurant to feed his chickens.

After paddling a canoe for four hours, Bill Sambola still has plenty of energy for wielding a machete to hack away the outer shell of coconuts to ready them for sale as refreshing pipas.

The Bogue Today

For the most part, the attitudes of the families who have lived in Tortuguero for generations have evolved with the times.

Their tongues may occasionally long to savor the flavor of a good turtle stew, but intellectually they recognize that they can live better by not eating the turtles. Turtles bring the tourists, and tourists bring the money that allows the village to not only survive but thrive.

The turtles, however, didn't bring the first tourists to Tortuguero—the fish did. Giant tarpon and snook drew a few hardy fishermen when turtles were still a menu item. But once the turtle station was in operation, Dr. Carr and the CCC began bringing people to Tortuguero to see for themselves the overharvesting and the critical decline of the turtle population. Arribadas of scientists, politicians, environmentalists, and journalists descended from tiny aircraft, where they'd been packed in with bedding, ice, beer, and other local necessities. They were willing to endure difficult travel and primitive living conditions just to see twentieth-century descendants of an ancient species drag themselves onto the beach to lay their eggs.

Lauren Murdock and Trevor Bringloe of New Brunswick, Canada, relax on Miss Junie's balcony. The two young biologists were drawn to Tortuguero by the prospect of seeing nesting turtles.

Carr told the people of Turtle Bogue that many other visitors would come for the turtles if the village welcomed and accommodated them. For the people of Tortuguero, nesting turtles were not unusual or special—they had always been there. Turtles were dinner and a source of income. As the village reached out to the trickle of specialists arriving with Dr. Carr, however, they saw that outsiders found something special and exciting in the turtles. And they began to believe

129

Turning Turtles

Tortuguero now boasts a small market, and though guaro is no longer delivered weekly, cases of beer are brought in by the boat load.

Carr's prophecy that the turtles could provide sustenance for the village without going the way of the soup pot. Slowly tourism began to grow, and the villagers adapted to take advantage of the new source of income. Turtles are still the focal point of the tourist industry, but the tropical environment and the abundant birdlife draw visitors year round.

Many of the villagers, like their parents, have lived their entire lives in Tortuguero. They have a strong sense of place—of home. They were practically born with canoe paddles in their hands; they respect but do not fear the limitations and dangers of the waterways and the jungles of their land. They learn early not to walk under the coconut trees, and they're taught at a young age where the crocodiles hang out. The older residents have fond memories of Archie and Marjorie Carr, Larry Ogren and Harry Hirth, and the Carr children. The stories have passed through the generations until some of the younger ones, who never really knew Carr-the-man, have almost deified Carr-the-savior of turtles and the village, speaking in hushed tones of the great Dr. Carr and his good works. Dr. Carr was no god, but he respected the people of Tortuguero and was concerned about their needs as well as those of the turtles.

Most of the residents of the village are involved in one way or another with the tourist trade. Ecotourism has also brought new residents to the village to take advantage of the influx of money, and there is some resentment of the newcomers. The old-timers say the outsiders come only for

Some things haven't changed. The coconuts on Miss Junie's property are still harvested by climbing the tall palms.

THE DOWNSIDE OF ECOTOURISM

Ecotourism is not a clearly defined term, and the intent of idealistic early promoters can easily become distorted. The practice usually begins with guides bringing small groups into ecologically sensitive areas to learn about, photograph, and enjoy the beauty of a pristine ecosystem. Serving the needs of these visitors also means income for area residents, and that is a good thing. Communities such as Tortuguero, impoverished only a generation ago, are thriving because of ecotourism. Then growth happens. It is only natural that as word spreads, more and more visitors want to come. The community must expand accordingly, and outsiders move in to take advantage of the opportunities. Campsites and rustic cabins lose ground to bigger and more luxurious accommodations.

Eventually, the operation is no longer ecotourism. It is just tourism. The environment is being degraded, resources are being used up, and the miracles of nature that initially brought people to the area are diminished. The balance that allows both the community and the environment to benefit is very delicate and must be constantly monitored.

Sales of tickets to Tortuguero National Park have grown from a few hundred a year after the park opened in the early 1970s to 117,341 in 2012 Costa Rica is trying hard to profit from tourism without destroying the very things that draw the tourists. To make the enterprise work, there must be cooperation from governments, businesses, and individuals, as well as constant oversight.

---

the easy money—they don't understand the history of the village or its ways.

Poaching continues to be a problem in the Bogue. Some like to blame the newcomers, who are not concerned with the long term. But Karla Taylor says the problem is bigger than that, observing that both long-time residents and newcomers play a role. The day before Mary and I arrived, there had been a demonstration to protest the lack of sufficient park rangers to protect the turtles. Karla said, with sadness in her voice, that the protesters were drawn mostly from her family and the biologists at the station. Some people still just don't understand.

The death in 2013 of Jairo Mora Sandoval introduces another grim note, suggesting that Costa Rica is not immune from the lawlessness that plagues other Central American countries. Although the murder, and the kidnappings that preceded it, did not occur in Turtle Bogue, the fate of the young conservationist serves as a reminder that turtle poaching is still serious business.

The Park

Walking along Tortuguero's main street, you pass a house offering mud boots for rent, cross a footbridge, and enter Tortuguero National Park. The path takes you to the park office located in what appears to be an old landlocked boat. Here you can pay the $10 entry fee and hike the muddy trails. A more comfortable way to see the park, however, is by boat. The park borders the lagoon and the sea and is networked with rivers, creeks, and canals. The canals date from the days when timber was being harvested in the rainforest and the logs were floated down the lagoon, and then on to the sawmill. You can take a boat from the village, where there are a variety of options, from canoes and kayaks to the open boats with seats for 12 to 18 passengers. The bigger boats are long and narrow—designed to navigate the narrow waterways of the park and provide easy viewing for passengers.

Open boats allow tourists a good view of the flora and fauna of the rainforest.

Whatever boat you choose, the trained eye of the guide spots wildlife that otherwise would blend in with the greens and browns of the rainforest. Alerted by a knowledgeable guide, you may suddenly find a mossy lump high in a tree peering back at you—it's a sloth, slowly turning its head to

Turning Turtles

This young sloth may be lost or may have just been making its way to the ground for its weekly toilet session when it found itself surrounded by a gaggle of turtle biologists. Can't a guy have a little privacy!

SLOTHS

Sloths can sometimes be spotted snugged into a tree fork or hanging upside down from a branch high in the rainforest canopy. But they are hard to see. They can remain very still for a long time, and green algae growing on their shaggy coats provides effective camouflage. Costa Rica has two species of sloth, the brown-throated, three-toed sloth and the Hoffmann's two-toed variety. Their slowness of movement and general inactivity can be attributed to a very slow digestive process. They must conserve energy! Many herbivores digest food within a few hours, but it may take a sloth many days to digest a single leaf.

Sloths spend most of their time in the canopy, but about once a week they make a slow descent to relieve themselves at the base of the tree. The sloth does not urinate or defecate in the meantime and therefore may expel as much as one-third of its body weight in a single visit to the ground. Biologists don't know why the sloth doesn't just poop from a tree limb and let it fall.

check out the activity below. Monkeys chase each other through the trees—three species, Geoffroy's spider monkey, mantled howler, and white-faced capuchin—live in the park. Near the boat, caiman, crocodiles, and river otters searching for a meal blend seamlessly into the water plants in response to the disturbance. Iguanas up to 5 feet long, sun themselves on tree limbs or on the bank, and exquisite birds are everywhere calling from the trees or fishing the shallows.

Tortuguero National Park was created in 1970 in order to protect the beach's green turtle nests, estimated at the time at 100,000 annually. It is by far the largest green turtle nesting beach in the Western Hemisphere. Archie Carr and his friend and ardent supporter Guillermo Cruz played an important role in the establishment of the 47,000-acre park that includes 22 miles of beach and extends approximately 18 miles into offshore waters. Though sea turtle conservation was a primary reason for establishing the park, its boundaries also protect 11 highly sensitive types of habitat. Tortuguero National Park can be reached only by air or water, but despite its isolation, it is the third most visited park in Costa Rica, with 117,341 paying visitors in 2012.

Turtle viewing in the park

During the day, canoes and other sightseeing boats come and go at will—as long as they stop at the park office each time to pay the $10 per person entrance fee. Turtle viewing, however, is much more strictly controlled. During turtle season, which runs from June through September, strictly regulated visits to see the nesting turtles are arranged under the auspices of the national park; when the sun goes down, visitors are not allowed on the beach except in the company of a certified guide. In 2012 an average of 221 people per night for a total of 28,537 people were authorized to go on turtle tours. Guides take pride in their certification and donate a portion of their earnings back to the community.

Tourists wait at a numbered path until a turtle is spotted, and the guide who is up next is directed to the numbered path closest to the nesting site.

Every night during the season, each guide is assigned by lottery an area of the beach and a time (8 p.m. or 10 p.m.). A guide may take up to 10 people in his time slot, with a maximum of 400 visitors allowed on the beach per night. The

Turning Turtles

A green turtle nests in the black sand of Tortuguero beach.

guide leads the little group along a sand track that follows the shoreline, stops in the designated area—and waits. Depending on nesting activity, you may be out for an hour or for several hours. It may be raining. The main path is separated from the beach by 15 feet or so of dense jungle, broken periodically by numbered paths that cut through to the beach. On a recent visit, my friend and I joined Noly's group in a slight drizzle and clustered on the main path, chatting quietly. We didn't have to wait long before a spotter on the beach contacted Noly, giving her a path number and the location of a turtle. Noly extinguished her small flashlight, and only her soft voice guided us as we concentrated on walking blind and staying upright in the mass of shifting sand.

As we approached our turtle, a group going the other way passed to our left. It was a moonless night, and we could only sense the others' presence as we moved in to replace them. They had watched the hen excavate a nest and were now being shuttled out of the way to make room for us. Noly sat by the big reptile's head, holding a small red-shaded light. Dr. Ehrenfeld's research had shown years ago that turtles do not see red light at all well, so we were able to look into the completed nest cavity, knowing that the turtle wasn't being disturbed. I dropped to the sand next to the turtle and watched raptly as the wet leathery eggs, glowing pink in the red light, dropped one by one, into the nesting cavity. I suppose the process lasted about 20 minutes.

When the last egg had been deposited, the light was extinguished, and we backed away to give the tired turtle room to complete her night's work. We sat in a tight group in the sand. We couldn't see each other or the turtle, but we could hear small sounds that told us she was filling the cavity, tamping it down, and throwing sand around to conceal the site. When she finished, still oblivious to our presence, she began dragging herself toward the sea. We followed—reverent attendants paying homage to a grande dame of Tortuguero and her timeless ritual.

TURNING TURTLES

Notes
Several quotations have been used from personal letters in Larry Ogren's private collection and have not been individually noted.

Introduction
1–Archie Carr, *The Sea Turtle: So Excellent a Fishe,* reissue ed. University of Texas Press, Austin 1984, p. 243

Chapter 1
2–Archie Carr, *The Windward Road: Adventures of a Naturalist on Remote Caribbean Shores*, reissue ed. Gainesville, University Press of Florida, 1979, p. 50–51
3–Larry Ogren, Letter to Dr. Archie Carr, August 20, 1956, Department of Special and Area Studies Collections, George A. Smathers Libraries, University of Florida
4–Edna Gail Dases, *A Place of Turtles: Reflections by Tio Leo Martinez, 2000,* unpublished.

Chapter 2
5–Archie Carr, *The Windward Road*, p. xxxii
6–David Ehrenfeld, *Beginning Again: People and Nature in the New Millennium*, Oxford University Press, 1993
7–Archie Carr, The *Windward Road*, p. xiv
8–Ibid
9–James Spotila, *Sea Turtles: A Complete Guide to Their Biology, Behavior, and Conservation*, Baltimore, The Johns Hopkins University Press and Oakwood Arts, 2004, p.8

Chapter 3
10–Harold Hirth, letter to Dr. Carr dated Friday, July 14, 1961, Smathers Libraries
11–Chuck Carr, (Archie Fairly Carr III) *Time Before*, unpublished essay

Chapter 4
13–Chuck Carr, *A Century of Sea Turtles*, Keynote presentation to The 20th Annual Sea Turtle Symposium, Orlando, FL March, 2000
14–Ibid

Chapter 5
15–Chuck Carr, *"Archie Carr, Model Naturalist,"* Conservation Biology, February 1997, Vol. 11, No. 1. Page 264.

Chapter 6
16 Sebastion Troeng, quoted by Julienne Gage, *Sebastian Troeng*, profile for *40 Under 40, International Development Leaders*,
http://dc40.devex.com/meet-the-40-under-40/sebastian-troeng/
17–Jeanne Mortimer, *Hawksbill Proposals are a Croc*, STC Press Release, April 13, 2000, conserveturtles.org.

Chapter 7
18–Edna Gail Dases, *A Place of Turtles: Reflections by Tio Leo Martinez, unpublished.*
19–Christopher P. Baker, Moon Travel Guides blog, June 20, 1911,
http://www.moon.com/blogs/cuba-costa-rica/choosing-personal-wilderness-guide-costa-rica

Sources and Suggested Reading

My central source was Larry Ogren through conversation and access to correspondence and papers both published and unpublished. Chuck Carr contributed generously of his time and unpublished writing. Other interviews included: Tom Carr, David Godfrey, Emma Harrison, Catalina González Prieto, David Ehrenfeld, James Spotila, and Karla Taylor. Much was gained from casual conversation with Miss Junie Taylor, other Tortuguero residents and STC staff in Costa Rica.

I mention here a selection of publications for further reading. Any of Archie Carr's books are a good read for the armchair naturalist or serious scientist. Two are specifically about sea turtles. *The Windward Road*, first published in 1956, has been reissued several times. *The Sea Turtle: So Excellent a Fishe*, first published in 1967 and reissued in 1984, tells about Carr's early turtle research and the field station at Tortuguero. James Spotila's book *Sea Turtles: A Complete Guide to Their Biology Behavior and Conservation* (Johns Hopkins University Press, 2004) is packed with good information and beautiful color photography. Spotila's *Saving Sea Turtles* (Johns Hopkins University Press, 2011) is a good read about conservationists dedicated to sea turtle preservation.

Harry Hirth (left), Leo Martinez (back), Durham Rankin (right), and an unidentified man in the far back release a batch of hatchlings recently hatched in the nursery.

Carl Safina's *Voyage of the Turtle: In Pursuit of the Earth's Last Dinosaur* (Henry Holt and Co., 2010) follows the life and travels of the giant leatherback. Frederick Rowe Davis details the life and work of Archie Carr in *The Man Who Saved Sea Turtles: Archie Carr and the Origins of Conservation Biology* (Oxford University Press, 2007). Two older books that were helpful are *The Green Turtle and Man*, James J. Parsons, University of Florida Press, 1962, and *Turtle Bogue: Afro-Caribbean Life and Culture in a Costa Rican Village*, Harry G. Lefever, *Susquehanna University Press, 1992*.

The sea turtle has become a conservation icon and there are many excellent books available. There are also many websites devoted all or in part to sea turtles including Sea Turtle Conservancy's extensive site.

Index

A

Ackerman, Ralph, 97
American Museum of Natural History, 40
American Philosophical Society, 40
American Society of Ichthyologists and Herpetologists, 33, 40
Archie Carr Center for Sea Turtle Research, 2
Archie Carr National Wildlife, Refuge, 11
Arribada, 31, 110
Ascension Island, 100, 101, 108, 118

B

Barra del Colorado, 16, 19, 36
Bjorndal, Karen A., 2, 11, 13, 43, 85, *106*, 107
Blanco, Juan Daniel Guerrero, *116*
Bringloe, Trevor, *129*
Brotherhood of the Green Turtle, 12, 40

C

Calipee, *32*, 34, 38, 39, 53, 99
Canneries, 25
Caribbean Conservation Corporation (CCC), 31, 40, 88, 103, 110, 111, 114, 129, see also, Sea Turtle Conservancy
Carr, Archie, 7–8, 11, 15–16, 22, *28*, 29–46, 47, 63, 69, 73, 79, *94*, 100, 103, 129,131
The Handbook of Turtles, 30
The Sea Turtle: So Excellent a Fishe, 13, 33, 138, 139
The Windward Road, 12, 13, 20, 33, 36, 37, 39, 40, 138, 139
World Sea Turtle Day, 12
Carr, Chuck, 4, *6*, *8*, 11, 13, *43*, 48, 50, 64, 65, 66, 67, 72, 73, 83, 84, 99, 99–101, 100, 101, *109*, 110, 127, 138, 139
Carr, David, 11, *109*–110
Carr, Marjorie Harris, 11, 43, *45*
Carr, Mimi, 11, 109
Carr, Stephen, 11, *44*, 109
Carr, Tom, 4, 11, 13, 43, *44*, 63, 64, 74, *109*, *110*, 139
Cayuca, 16, 18, 21, *26*, *54*, 55, 56, 60, 64, *67*, 70, 86, 112
Chelonia mydas, see *green sea turtle*
Churchill, Winston, 34
CITES, 7
Curry, Raymond, 94, *95*
Coconuts, 50, 60, 109, 124, *131*
Conservation Biology, 101, 105, 138, 139
Conu, Santiago, 58
Cruz, Guillermo (Billy), 30, 31, 38, *91*, 114, 134

D

Dases, Edna Gail, 26, 125, 138
Downs, Bertie, 15, 16,122

E

Ecotourism,132
Ehrenfeld, David, 13, 38, 43, 105, 109, 138, 139
Endangered Species Act, 6

Miss Junie prepares tamales for lunch.

Jeff Schmid PhD, of The Conservancy of Southwest Florida, a protegé of Larry Ogren's share's Archie Carr's fascination with in the Kemp's ridley. The Kemp's, the most seriously endangered sea turtles almost disappeared. Prior to the April, 2010 oil spill in the Gulf of Mexico, it had made a remarkable recovery. However, after the spill, more dead Kemp's ridleys than any other turtle were collected. Because of the slow growth and maturity rate, it will be many years before the full impact of the spill can be accessed. Jeff's graph below shows how the population plunged from the huge arribadas of the 1940s to almost zero, then thanks to conservation efforts slowly began to rebuild.

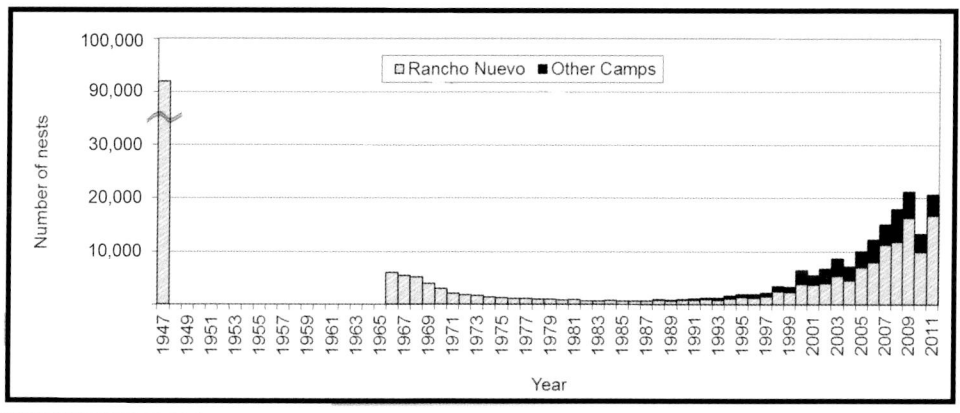

F

Fernandez, Juanita, *126*
José Figueres Ferrer (Don Pepe), 31, 38, 39, 41
Forest, 23
Frick, Jane, 83

G

Garcia, Eliza Alvin, *126*
Giovannolli, Leonard, 10, 22, 73
Godfrey, David 2, 4, 111, 139
Green sea turtle (*Chelonia mydas*), 10, 12, 14, *15, 24,* 34, 37, *38,* 45, 53, *68,* 69, *75, 76, 78, 80, 85, 92, 97,* 107, *117,* 115, 116, 134, *136, 137*
Griffing, Brenda, 4
Gup, Ted, 2, 4

H

Harrison, Tom, 74
Harrison, Emma 4, 113, *139*
Hawksbill (*Eretmochelys imbricata*) 32, 34, 36 77,, 107, 108, 115
Hernández, Noel Lau, 116, *118,* 121, 139
Hirth, Harry, 11, 13, *35,* 43, *63,* 64, 66, 78, *88,* 96, 103, 105, 127, 131

I

International Union for the Conservation of Nature and Natural Resources (IUCN) 41, 108

141

TURNING TURTLES

Larry sent this cartoon to his colleagues at NMFS an inside joke for the benefit of enforcement agents who had the hard work of dealing with poachers and looking for ways to bust them.

K

Kemp's ridley (*Lepidochelys kempii*), 31, 33, 110

L

La Pavona, 121
Leatherback *(Dermochelys coriacca)*, 22, 26, 78, 98, 102, 115, 116, 119, 139

M

Marine Turtle Specialist Group, 41, 108
Martinez, Leo, 13, *26*, 27, 43, 49, 52, *53*, *56*, 57, 58, 59, *60*, 63, *64*, 65, 66, 67, *70,* 71, 92, 99, *101*, 102, 112, 114, 122, 124, 125, 138

Martinez, Obid, 71, 125
Martinez, Shefton, *28, 49,* 83
Martinez, Sibella, 13, 37, 50, *51*, 50–67, 51, 61, 64
Martinez, Walton, 124
Meylan, Anne, 13, 43, *107*, 108
Montalbán, Chico, 50, *54*, 114
Mortimer, Jeanne, 13, 108, 138
Murdock, Lauren, *129*

N

National Science Foundation, 32
Nuñez, Xavier, 56

O

Ocampos, Indira Torrez,*118*
Ogren, Kim, 4
Larry Ogren, 6, 11, 12, 13, *14,* 15–24, *35*, 41, *43, 45, 46,*47–64, *58, 70, 72,* 74, 78, 80, 80–82, *87, 88, 90, 101,* 96, 102, 102–105, 109, *110,* 111, 122, 131
Oliver, Jim, 40
Operation Green Turtle (OGT), 40, *85*–96,

P

Panamerican Agricultural School, 30
Phipps, John H., 40, 42, 87, 111
Popenoe, Wilson, 30
Prieto, Catalina González, 114, 139
Pritchard, Peter, 13, 43

R

Rats, 48, 57, 63
Rosenthal, Alan, 114

S

Sambola, Bill, 54, 67, *120*, 127, *128,* 139
Martinez, Sam, 22, 25
Sandoval, Jairo Mora, 98, 132
Satelite transmitters, 117
Sawmill, *23*
Schroeder, Robert, 68
Scott, Peter, 41
Sea Turtle Conservancy (STC), 2, 40, see also *Caribbean Conservation Corp.*
Sea turtle eggs, 2, 22, 30, 31, 32, 33, 34, 35, 39, 49, 53, 55, 59, 60, 65, 69, 70, 74, 75, 76, 77, 78, 79, 82, 88, 93, 97, 108, 115, 116, 129, 136
Silman, Roxana, 113
Sloths, 18, *134*
Sotherland, Paul, 98
Spotila, James 13, 44, 98, 105, 138, 139

T

Tagging Data, 115, 118
Taylor, Albert, *46*, 54
Taylor, Byron, 122
Taylor, Cleoid, 126
Taylor, Dorling, 13, 122, 126, 139
Taylor, Karla, 126, *127*, 128, 132, 139
Taylor, Miss Junie, 13, 46, 121, 122, 124, *125*, 126, 127, 128, 129, 131, 139
Taylor, Noly, 126, 136
TEDs 104–105
Thieme, Mary, 4, 13, 121, 127, 128, 132
Torres, Randall, 113, 139
Tortuguero National Park, 39, 132, 133, 134, 135
Tour de Turtles, 119
Troeng, Sebastian, 111, 138

U

U.S. National Marine Fisheries Service, 12
U.S. Navy, 19, 40, 86, 87

V

Valverde, Roldán, 2, 4
Vanoli, Francisco, 18
Veladors, 24, 34

W

Wildlife Conservation Society, 109
Wing, Jim, 58

Photo credits

All photos copyrighted to the respective contributers.
All cartoons © Larry Ogren.
Photos are listed by the contributor and page number.

Foreword
Anne Ake: P 6
Sea Turtle Conservancy (STC): P 8

Chapter 1
All photos in Chapter 1 are from Larry Ogren's collection.

Chapter 2
STC: pp 28, 29, 36, 38, 42, 45 (top)
Department of Special and Area Studies Collections, George A. Smathers Libraries, University of Florida: pp 32, 36
Larry Ogren: pp 35, 43, 45 (bottom)
Tom Carr: pp 44

Chapter 3
All photos in Chapter 3 are from Larry Ogren's collection

Chapter 4
Larry Ogren: pp 70, 71, 78, 80
STC: pp 75, 76, 85
Robert Schroeder: p 68

Chapter 5
All photos in chapter 1 are from Larry Ogren's collection.

Chapter 6
Larry Ogren: p 102
Anne Ake: pp 104, 110, 112 (bottom), 113, 114, 115, 118
STC: pp 109, 112 (middle), 117
Smathers: 106, 112 (top)
Anne Meylan: p 107

Chapter 7
STC: p 136
Schroeder: p 137
Anne Ake: all other photos

Back Matter
STC: pp 139, 140
Jeff Schmid: p 141
Elaine Anderson: p 144

Turning Turtles

Village People:

Two men take a break on remnants of the old saw mill.

Three children huddle on a playground bench.

A boy and his chicken.

All is pura vida.

T

Tagging Data, 115, 118
Taylor, Albert, *46*, 54
Taylor, Byron, 122
Taylor, Cleoid, 126
Taylor, Dorling, 13, 122, 126, 139
Taylor, Karla, 126, *127*, 128, 132, 139
Taylor, Miss Junie, 13, 46, 121, 122, 124, *125*, 126, 127, 128, 129, 131, 139
Taylor, Noly, 126, 136
TEDs 104–105
Thieme, Mary, 4, 13, 121, 127, 128, 132
Torres, Randall, 113, 139
Tortuguero National Park, 39, 132, 133, 134, 135
Tour de Turtles, 119
Troeng, Sebastian, 111, 138

U

U.S. National Marine Fisheries Service, 12
U.S. Navy, 19, 40, 86, 87

V

Valverde, Roldán, 2, 4
Vanoli, Francisco, 18
Veladors, 24, 34

W

Wildlife Conservation Society, 109
Wing, Jim, 58

Photo credits

All photos copyrighted to the respective contributers.
All cartoons © Larry Ogren.
Photos are listed by the contributor and page number.

Foreword
Anne Ake: P 6
Sea Turtle Conservancy (STC): P 8

Chapter 1
All photos in Chapter 1 are from Larry Ogren's collection.

Chapter 2
STC: pp 28, 29, 36, 38, 42, 45 (top)
Department of Special and Area Studies Collections, George A. Smathers Libraries, University of Florida: pp 32, 36
Larry Ogren: pp 35, 43, 45 (bottom)
Tom Carr: pp 44

Chapter 3
All photos in Chapter 3 are from Larry Ogren's collection

Chapter 4
Larry Ogren: pp 70, 71, 78, 80
STC: pp 75, 76, 85
Robert Schroeder: p 68

Chapter 5
All photos in chapter 1 are from Larry Ogren's collection.

Chapter 6
Larry Ogren: p 102
Anne Ake: pp 104, 110, 112 (bottom), 113, 114, 115, 118
STC: pp 109, 112 (middle), 117
Smathers: 106, 112 (top)
Anne Meylan: p 107

Chapter 7
STC: p 136
Schroeder: p 137
Anne Ake: all other photos

Back Matter
STC: pp 139, 140
Jeff Schmid: p 141
Elaine Anderson: p 144

143

Turning Turtles

Village People:

Two men take a break on remnants of the old saw mill.

Three children huddle on a playground bench.

A boy and his chicken.

All is pura vida.